GOOD NEWS
Thoughts on God and Man

GOOD NEWS

Thoughts on God
and Man by

J. B. Phillips

WIPF & STOCK · Eugene, Oregon

Wipf and Stock Publishers
199 W 8th Ave, Suite 3
Eugene, OR 97401

Good News
Thoughts on God and Man
By Phillips, J. B.
Copyright©1963 SCM
ISBN 13: 978-1-62032-319-9
Publication date 6/1/2012
Previously published by SCM, 1963

CONTENTS

	PREFACE	vii
	INTRODUCTION	1
I.	THE PURPOSE OF GOD	13
II.	FAITH	69
III.	HOPE	97
IV.	LOVE	129
V.	THE CHRISTIAN YEAR	157

ACKNOWLEDGEMENTS

I AM grateful to the Editors of the *Church of England Newspaper*, the *Church Times*, *The Life of Faith* and the *Methodist Recorder* for their freely-given permission to reproduce matter which first appeared in their periodicals.

The chapter on Hope which begins on p. 97, was originally a broadcast talk and subsequently appeared in a slightly different form in *New Testament Christianity*. I am grateful to Messrs. Hodder & Stoughton for their permission to reproduce this and a few sentences which have appeared in *God Our Contemporary*.

I should also like to thank the Reverend Norman J. Bull (Senior Lecturer at St. Luke's College, Exeter) for editing my work.

Swanage, Dorset.   J. B. PHILLIPS

PREFACE

I BELIEVE that it is high time for the word "Gospel" to be rehabilitated. It is a fine strong word with an interesting ancestry. Back in the days of Homer the Greek word *euaggelion* meant the reward given to the bringer of good news. Then its meaning changed over the centuries to denote, not the reward, but the good news itself. It was ripe for adoption by the New Testament writers, who invested it with a special importance. Instead of meaning any sort of good news, it was used to mean the Good News of God, the Christian Gospel. And with that specialised meaning it came into our language through the Old English god-spel.

But in common speech in latter years the special meaning of the word has been blurred by loose usage. It is employed to mean almost any kind of teaching, ideal, remedy or programme. Thus we may read of the "gospel" of hard work, the "gospel" of success, the "gospel" of a salt-free diet or even the "gospel" of Communism. I feel that the word needs rescuing before it is further debased.

In Christian circles we must see that what purports to be the Christian Gospel is always, and in the best sense, Good News. It is not good news, for example, for a man to be told that he is a hell-deserving sinner; but it is good news for him to be told that he need no longer feel guilty and afraid towards God, and can begin here and now to live as God's son. The stimulation of the guilt-sense in sensitive people can never be the proclamation of good news; and neither can the attempt to perpetuate an image of God who is either Church-bound or Bible-bound, or both. Such distortions cause untold damage to the human spirit, and create a dozen rebels for every convert. A great many people repudiate what has been put before them as the Christian Gospel: they have never been able to see how good is the true Good News.

Reduced to its simplest possible terms the Good News is simply that God is Love. And this statement, although it sounds like a wild over-simplification, is in fact the enormously compressed kernel of all truth. Of course the minister of the Gospel must expand the basic fact. He must show the sort of God whom Christians worship. He must communicate his own conviction that God, despite his silence and invisibility, is more real than the passing things which we see and handle. He must emphasise that God, though we know him to be infinitely greater than our most far-seeing grandparents could ever imagine, yet entered the arena of human life to teach, to suffer and to die. He must plainly state that the reconciliation between God and man (which all the great religions recognise as a prime necessity), was made in the Person of Jesus Christ. And he must further teach that this same God, who focused himself in a human being, has destroyed the power of man's last enemy, death. Indeed he must proclaim that all the guilts and fears which torment men's souls have been removed potentially by God's initiative, and can be removed actually by his active contemporary Spirit. To tell of a God who is not merely Supreme Mind but a God who cares with infinite compassion for individual people is to proclaim Good News.

Now life contradicts this fact at every turn; at any rate it *appears* to do so. The wicked prosper, the undeserving suffer, and little can be discerned of "one increasing purpose". Yet the Good News must be proclaimed in spite of appearances, in spite of setbacks and disasters, for it is the basic truth of the universe. It is not affected by the ebb and flow of human circumstance. Its centre of gravity is not in this planet at all, and never has been considered to be so by thinking Christians. Certainly the joy and power of the young Church was largely due to the fact that those early heroic members of the Kingdom of God knew that they had here no continuing city. Since the prevalent modern mental attitude is desperately earth-bound it becomes more and more important for the proclaimer of the Good News to emphasise that the things which are seen are temporal but the things which are not seen are eternal. Let a man give his heart to God and give this passing world no greater loyalty than it deserves, and he knows a peace which passes understanding. He does not become, as some might suppose, a man so preoccupied with other-worldly things that he cares not at all for his fellows who live in this transitory world. We have only to look at the record of true Christians in all centuries. Who cares most for the poor, the weak, the blind, the crippled, the deaf and dumb and every other victim of the human predicament? Always in the forefront of works of compassion will be found the man who has accepted the Good News with heart and mind. As God loves him, so he attempts to love his fellows.

The contents of this book are concerned with various aspects of the central message of Good News. But I confess I often wonder at that curious human frailty which is reluctant to believe good news simply because it *is* good. It may be a kind of acquired caution; it may be that life has taught us that simple solutions are usually false solutions. But it is disturbing to find that a childlike acceptance of what is really and truly God's Good News is quite rare. Sometimes, and especially in the sensitive, it is our own consciences which are overscrupulous; we find it almost impossible to believe that God can be more merciful to us than we are ourselves. Sometimes it is simply a matter of our old arch-enemy, Pride. We are prepared to lash ourselves and sweat away along some supposed road to salvation, but to accept what the New Testament asserts with startling candour is "God's free gift" is an affront to our precious sense of achievement. I believe that if this were some human panacea for our ills, or some human blueprint for our conduct, our suspicions and our reluctance might well be justified. But this, the Good News, is a revelation of the initiative of God, so simple that the humblest can grasp its meaning and yet so unfathomable in its mysterious effects that the wise may spend a lifetime in contemplating its significance. Good news is surely not to be rejected merely because it *is* good!

Let us also be on our guard against that common human tendency to elaborate a simple issue. Compare, for example, the directness of Christ's words to the thief on the cross, "today shalt thou be with me in Paradise", or Paul's plain statement that death only means "to be with Christ, which is far better", with the enormous over-elaboration of Newman's Dream of Gerontius. Yet Newman's work is greatly admired, while Paul's conviction is scarcely taken seriously. I also believe that we who call ourselves Christians should be continually vigilant against those who would darken counsel by complicating the simplicity of our faith. We need to beware even of the religious books we read, or before long the simple walk with God becomes such a complicated spiritual exercise that the Good News ceases to be good. I do not claim that Christianity is easy; I do claim that it is not complicated. The application of the Christian faith to our common life may indeed tax our best brains, but the central life that is lived in fellowship with God is not, and I am sure was never meant to be, complicated.

Seven years ago, on the advice of two Bishops, I left the parochial life of the Church of England, since the burden of translating the New Testament in addition to the duties of a parish priest were proving too exacting. This temporary "retirement" enabled me not only to continue my work of translation, but to travel many thousands of miles in England and in Scotland to address groups of all denominations except the Roman Catholic. I received a warm welcome from every denomination, and I became more and more convinced that the things upon which Christians agree are very much greater than those on which they differ. In common honesty I could not deny, even if I wished, that the same Holy Spirit is at work in all the churches. This has been a stimulating as well as an exhausting experience, and various friends have suggested that some of the talks which I have given during my travels might be edited and put into a more permanent form. They make up part of this book.

But in addition to addressing groups which varied from a packed (Presbyterian) Cathedral in Edinburgh to a small but enthusiastic Salvation Army branch meeting, from a large group of American airmen stationed in this country to a girls' public school, I have been able to do a certain amount of broadcasting both for the B.B.C. and for the Australian Broadcasting Commission. The latter broadcast talks have not been heard in this country, and they, with two or three B.B.C. broadcasts, have been included in this volume.

I have been further able to write articles for various periodicals, in particular for the *Church Times*, the *Church of England Newspaper*, the *Methodist Recorder* and *The Life of Faith*. Each of these articles reached a comparatively small public and, again on the advice of my friends, they are included here. For it is not very likely that an article which appeared in the *Church Times* was read by many Methodists, Baptists or Congregationalists. And, to speak the truth in love, it is even less likely that an article which appeared in the *Methodist Recorder* or *The Life of Faith* would catch the eye of the average reader of the *Church Times*!

It has thus seemed to me that it might be useful to bring together in one volume addresses, sermons, broadcasts and articles which I have produced over the last few years. They are all directly connected with the Good News which I, like every other clergyman and minister, am commissioned to preach.

Readers will notice how many passages I have quoted from my *New Testament in Modern English* (Geoffrey Bles) and how useful they are in communicating the Good News.

INTRODUCTION

Quality and Quantity

I SHOULD think that everybody, unless he happens to be very stupid indeed, knows the difference between quality and quantity. Of course, quantity can be impressive. An enormous number of anything, whether it's bushels of wheat, or books, or human beings, *is* impressive. But most of us are concerned not with the impressiveness of numbers, but with the quality of what we produce or buy. If you are furnishing your home or your farm, or perhaps buying a present for a special friend, what is chiefly in your mind is not the number of things that you can purchase, but their quality. In fact, most people have sufficient good sense to buy the best quality they can afford, not only because it gives more pleasure to the eye or the ear, but because in sober fact the better the quality the better value you get for your money. This not only applies to the business of our ordinary living, but it also applies to our hobbies and recreations. Whether it's a gun or a fishing-rod, a tennis racquet, a pair of shoes or a dancing-frock, we go for the best quality that we can afford.

Now although most of us are wide awake to the difference between quantity and quality in things, I don't think we are nearly so sensible in our judgement about people. We're far more impressed than we ought to be by the quantity of a man's gifts, and sometimes we are slow to appreciate the quality, or lack of it, in his life. For instance, it's only too easy to be dazzled by a man who's a clever talker, possesses that indefinable something that we call "charm", has plenty of drive, is good at games and is what is called a "good mixer", and never see that he has got all his goods in the shop-window. We may fail to see that the real quality of his life is poor and shallow. And indeed, as long as he gets away with it, the poor chap may not see it himself.

Now Jesus Christ, whose insight was always accurate and sometimes very disturbing, invariably went straight to the root of the matter. To him what really mattered was not the number of a man's gifts, but what sort of person that man was. To him it was quality that mattered and not window-dressing. He says it quite plainly: "The quality of a man's life is nothing to do with the number of his possessions."

What Sort of Person am I?

Now you may think this is all very obvious, but it really isn't, you know. The ordinary current judgements of the world are very often based on a man's outward possessions. People say, "He's worth so many thousands", or "He owns so many thousand acres", or "He's written a best-seller", or "He's very popular on the radio", and treat the man with respect and admiration in consequence. In fact, the quality of the man's life may be very poor, spiritually; he may have little or no knowledge of God, and no spiritual resources to draw on if things go wrong for him. Jesus rightly insists that what really matters is quality. What sort of person are you? In the eyes of God – that is, in Reality – that is always what matters. God is not impressed by our gifts (which are his anyway!) or by our bank balance, which is a purely temporary affair of this world, in any case. But he is always concerned with what sort of persons we are.

Now suppose you were to ask yourself in all honesty this simple question: "What sort of person am I?" I don't mean, "What do I possess?", and I don't mean, "What have I achieved?" and I certainly don't mean, "What sort of impression have I made on other people?" But I do mean, "What am I in the eyes of God – what sort of quality do I possess in my inward life?"

I think, if the truth were told, a great many people would have to admit that they are very far from satisfied with themselves. They may still have their ideals, but it is uncomfortably true that they don't live up to them. They may know what they ought to be, but that is very different from what they actually are. Many people keep themselves very busy not only to gain money and prestige, but simply to avoid facing this unpleasant contrast. It's far easier to reflect comfortably upon all our busyness or the number of our possessions than to think honestly about what sort of people we are.

Some time ago I was listening on the radio to a debate broadcast from Cambridge University on the motion that "Modern Youth is not worthy of its heritage". Of course, like all university debates, it was light-hearted and full of funny remarks, and made very good listening. But the burden of the argument seemed to be that modern youth has been handed on such a messy and difficult heritage that it could not fail to be more than worthy of such a poor thing! If this had been a serious debate, I should have felt very tempted to ask: "If it is true that you have been handed such a ghastly muddle as a heritage, what makes you think you will have done any better when the time comes for your sons to debate the question?" For, funnily enough, I was at Cambridge University soon after the first World War, and I can remember almost that identical question being discussed, and the same conclusion being reached – that it was the previous generation which was to blame.

Good News

Now the plain and obvious fact is that if we want a better world, better in every sense, we not only want fair dealings and just laws, but we need *better quality people*. For this, whether we like it or not, is where so many human ideas and ideals break down.

People just haven't got sufficient inward resources to make the ideas and ideals come true.

I ask you then to notice afresh the profound wisdom of Jesus Christ. He doesn't deal with outward regulations, but with a continual insistence on a change of heart. In fact, He says: "You cannot have good fruit without a good tree". And if I read his mind aright, his hope for the world lies in "making the tree good". In other words, in changing the inner quality of people's lives.

People often say, either cynically or resignedly, that "you cannot change human nature". And indeed it's perfectly true that if you study the lives of people of thousands of years ago, you'll find that they are essentially much the same as we are. But the whole point of Christ's teaching, the whole reason why Christianity is GOOD NEWS, is that essential human nature *can* be transformed, not by rules and regulations, but by an inward change of loyalty. The Kingdom of God, that is, the recognition by all men everywhere of God's sovereignty, and the willingness of all men everywhere to co-operate with his high purpose, remains an idle dream unless there is this inner change-over. Words like "conversion" and "repentance" have often been spoiled for us, either because they have been made to mean the wrong things, or because we have heard them too often. But if you read the Gospels you will see that what Jesus means by "repentance" or being "converted" is a change of inward attitude. Once the inner loyalty of a man's life is fundamentally changed, we can expect an enormous improvement in quality. But so long as the life, however respectable, remains self-centred and regulated by the values of this world, there won't be any spontaneous love and goodwill and hope and courage and faith, and all the other things that the world so desperately needs. These things have got to grow naturally from a heart whose inner loyalty has been changed. Otherwise they're as unnatural and useless as sticking a dead branch into the ground and tying fruit to it with string!

If we are honest, we realise the spiritual poverty of our innermost lives. We produce certain goodnesses from time to time by a certain amount of effort, but unless we are real and honest Christians at heart we don't produce spontaneously what St. Paul rightly called "the fruits of the Spirit". We are powerless to do much to improve the quality of our lives without the help of Christ.

Better Quality People

We can, of course, do something by our own efforts. We can learn to discipline ourselves. We have the ability to choose whether our lives are completely self-centred, or whether they are really given to the best interests of our fellow-men. Up to a point, then, we can do something, and if we have been lucky enough to have had a sensible Christian upbringing there will be quite a lot of good things that we do almost automatically. Yet I am certain that for most people, if there is to be any real and lasting change of quality of living, they need someone *outside themselves* to help them. The direction of our lives, and therefore their quality, will depend on what in our heart of hearts we love, and on what in our heart of hearts we really believe. Left to ourselves we very quickly run out of ideals, we get infected with the spirit of the world around us, and we lose a sense of purpose – in fact, before very long, we make a sort of working compromise. Yet we know very well that our lives are not of the sort of quality that we should like them to be.

What, to be perfectly simple, we really need is someone to believe in, someone to command our adult love, big enough to command our loyalty, respect and worship. We need to get to know the one who is in charge of the whole enormously complex human activity we call Life, so that we can co-operate with his purpose. All this remains vague and beyond our reach until we accept the infinite God focused in the person of Christ. In him, we find not only the highest possible quality of living, but we find that if we transfer our faith from ourselves to him that we begin to understand God, we begin to see something of the purpose of God and our part in that purpose. This is tremendously important of course, for a life without a master-loyalty is like a ship without either compass or rudder. But there is more to it than simply finding the answer to our human craving for a master-loyalty. We find, as thousands have found, that through Christ the resources of God can be tapped and, incredible as it may sound, something of God's own quality of living becomes available for us.

At the risk of repeating myself, I feel I must put this to you once again, for it is the very heart and essence of the Christian Gospel. If you and I, ordinary people in all sorts of different circumstances, are to become better quality people, we cannot make much headway without the help of God. God remains a vast and unknowable mystery until we accept that planned focusing of himself in Christ, who actually lived a human life of which we have reliable records, and who is alive today. Moreover, the Spirit of Christ, the Spirit of God, the Holy Spirit – the name is not important – is immediately available to transform and reinforce the lives of those who want to follow Christ's way of living. By this faith in the revealed God, that is, in Christ, and by the opening of their hearts to him, men can find a permanent and effective improvement in the quality of their living. This has been proved times without number, and it is GOOD NEWS.

What about Sin?

Now you may be saying to yourself: "But he hasn't said a word about sin and forgiveness, still less has he used the familiar religious terms such as 'justification' and 'sanctification'." I know that very well, and I shall have a word to say about sin and forgiveness in a moment. But it seems to me that some Christian preachers quite often start at the wrong end. They try with all their power to convince people of the depth of their sin. Yet it is very remarkable, and I would ask you to notice this particularly, that this is a method almost never used by Jesus Christ. His way was to call people to follow him, to follow his way of life, and to share his quality of living. I think he knew very well that people who sincerely try to do this would discover quite quickly enough their own selfishness and sinfulness. He doesn't appear to have made a fuss about this, although he warned people that following his way, though it contained the secret of joy and peace, would certainly have its pains and difficulties. After all, if you think about it, if a man means business where God is concerned and is prepared to follow the way of Christ, he won't need me or anybody else to tell him of his own weakness and sinfulness. He'll very quickly find out that although the new way of living is enormously attractive and desirable, yet the pull of his old habit and the force of his love for himself is pretty strong.

Now I don't see the sense of being morbid over this, or of paying it too much attention. The more you weep and wail over your sins, and possibly brood over them, the bigger they loom in your mind and the more hold they are likely to have over you. Suppose we take all that for granted and concentrate instead on the boundless resources which become available to us through Christ. To my mind Christians pay far too much attention to the fact of sin and far too little to the possibilities of becoming and living like sons of God, which is what the New Testament promises. When Paul spoke of being "strengthened with might by his Spirit in the inner man", for example, I am perfectly certain he wasn't spinning words; he was speaking of actual and realisable experience. In dozens and dozens of places he writes of the shining possibilities of inward transformation by the Spirit of the living God. Surely it is far better to think of these, and believe that they are capable of becoming true in our own lives, than to spend time moping over our unworthiness and sinfulness. This is where the battle really lies, *to believe that God is thoroughly capable of transforming and empowering us.* Appearances, past failures, feelings, all sorts of things may try to deprive us of really believing in the resources of God. *And this is where we must fight*; and indeed as far as I can recollect the only battle we are ever told to wage in the New Testament is to fight the good fight of faith. We only tarnish the shining promises of God if we persist in dwelling on our own sinfulness.

New Life

Now that we've got things in perspective we can turn to the matter of forgiveness. And let's say straight away, quite plainly and honestly, that there is nothing in the world we can do to *earn* or *deserve* our forgiveness. It is a part of the Love of God that we simply have to accept, humbly and gratefully, but not cringingly or morbidly. I believe with all my heart that Christ made the only possible reconciliation between selfish humanity and the Perfection of God, but I cannot see that he either did or does demand from people that they accept a certain theory of Atonement, for instance, before they can be his friends or co-operators. In his quiet but strangely compelling invitation to "follow him", and share the new quality of living, is included the gift of full and free forgiveness for the past. Probably we *shall* want to tell him that we are sorry for the self-centredness, for the pain and harm we have caused to other people as well as to him. But having said this honestly, he wants us, I am sure, to go forward, to learn a new way of living, which forgets about self and pride and reputation and success, and gives its whole loyalty to him. That way, and that way alone, lies the life of good quality – satisfying, creative living. It is, in fact, quite simply what the New Testament call "eternal life" – the privilege of sharing by us, little creatures as we are, in the timeless life of God.

I

THE PURPOSE OF GOD

Worship

TO WORSHIP, that is to "see the worth" of something outside ourselves, is a normal human activity. Whether people are religious or not, almost everybody pours out love, admiration, devotion, the willingness to serve and make sacrifices for, somebody or something, and that, naturally, *is* worship. The object of a man's worship may be a football team, it may be a "pop" singer, a film or TV star. In fact it may be anybody who has skill or strength or talent or artistic ability beyond his own, and that calls forth feelings of worship.

Now whatever we worship is bound to make a great difference to the sort of people we are. Our whole character and outlook is moulded, not by what we *profess* to worship but by what in fact we *do* worship, and we must be very honest with ourselves about it. The chief enemies of Jesus Christ, for example, were ostensibly worshipping God. But in fact, as Jesus continually pointed out to them, they were worshipping such things as power, privilege, position, wealth and success. It's because worshipping the wrong things produces the wrong kind of people that Jesus spoke so sternly. And it's for that reason that the whole Bible so roundly condemns the worship of "false gods". It is, then, of the utmost importance for those of us who want to worship God that we should see something of his true greatness.

Modern man does not, I believe, worship the living God very much. This is partly because he is seduced and blinded by the gods of the modern age – Success, Prestige, Glamour, Money, Power and Security. Such things loom so large in his reading and thinking, yes, and in his viewing and listening, that he has become spiritually short-sighted.

Ideas of God

Apart from this, many people today find it difficult to hold a conception of God which they can honestly worship. I have talked with a good many people who don't believe in God, or who have given up faith in him. In most cases I find that such people have thrown overboard childish ideas of God, and have found nothing to put in their place. Of course it's very common for adolescents, who are working their way from dependence towards independence, to rebel against authority. And this is very often the time when the childish faith is thrown overboard along with everything else which is a reminder of childhood. But it is a tragedy if, after rejecting the childish, young people fail to discover a God great enough to command their adult worship and love. We don't expect the ideas and loyalties of childhood in any other department of life to have the same significance when we grow up. And yet to hear some people talk, you'd think that in advocating faith in God we were recommending a return to childhood! The truth is exactly the opposite – what we're trying to do is to get people to leave behind the childish and the inadequate, to look away from the distraction and false values of this world and to rediscover the living God.

God in Christ

I've become more and more convinced that if we are to find a personal God we must accept his planned focusing of himself in the man Jesus Christ. If we don't do this, we're left with such a vast and overpowering idea of the wisdom and complexity of the mind behind the universe that a personal God becomes impossible. Every good scientist feels a tremendous sense of awe and wonder as he discovers more and more of this amazing universe. But I don't believe that he discovers God as a person, not only infinite in his greatness, but infinite in his concern for the individual, until he accepts Jesus Christ as what he claimed to be. You may be moved to wonder and awe at the infinite mind behind all the things that we can observe, but you cannot easily love, worship and adore what is practically an abstraction! It's only when we see God expressed, as it were, in a human being, living under human conditions and limitations, that the idea of worship has any meaning.

Now let's be clear what we're saying. No Christian is claiming that the *whole* of God, so to speak, can be confined and compressed into one short human life, lived in Palestine some two thousand years ago. But what Christ himself claimed was to reveal the nature and character of God. So that if we accept his claim, however immense our conception of God may be, the clue to his nature and purpose will always be found in Christ. In other words, we look out upon that immense mystery which we call "God" through the opening which Christ has made in our darkness.

If we take the revelation of Christ seriously we may find we've been mistaken about the true greatness of God. As human beings, we're so made that we're bound to be impressed by size or great numbers, or by sheer power. And for this reason we tend to make in our minds images of God which are really no more than projections of man, enormously magnified in size, wisdom and power. Of course God *is* infinitely greater than we are, in wisdom and power and in everything else, but the greatness of God is not a matter of size!

The Weakness of God

There is, for example, his almost incredible humility. That quiet insertion of himself into human history, which we celebrate at Christmas-time, is not a piece of pious legend. It's a sober fact of history. Anyone with any imagination at all can think of some God of righteousness and power breaking through into the life of this sinful planet, in wrath and judgement, and displaying enough physical force to make the bravest tremble! *But that was not the way of God with whom we have to do.* He came not to condemn but to save, and his humble means of entry is a strong clue to his character. No man's freewill is interfered with; no man's personality is assaulted; no one is *forced* to do anything at all. God enters his world in humble circumstances, God lives life on the same terms as he expects all human beings to live it. God accepts no special privilege nor protection, and in the end God is betrayed and executed, without any superhuman intervention. On the face of it, it seems a weak and feeble intrusion into human affairs, and it's that *apparent* weakness which we must never forget.

For the methods of God have not changed. He is still gentle and humble and apparently weak. The self-centred girl can keep God at arms' length for as long as she wants, and the conceited man can do the same. It's a rather frightening thought, but it remains true that God does not interfere with anyone's freedom to choose. That's not to say that God is impotent and inoperative in his own world. He speaks, wherever men will listen, through conscience, through circumstance, and through the crying needs of other people. He's unceasingly calling people away from the life that leads to unhappiness and destruction to the life that leads to peace and co-operation with himself.

There's a wisdom at work here, higher than any of our wisdom. Two thousand years ago you'd have said that the life of the field-preacher Jesus was an insignificant failure. Yet today there are millions who gladly serve and worship him, and many who have proved their willingness to die for his sake. The greatness of Jesus, the greatness of our God, is quite different from the greatness which men usually admire.

Our Responsibility

I've already mentioned the very risky gift of free-will which God gives to us human beings, and with which he doesn't interfere. We all have a personal responsibility in moral decision, which we cannot honestly evade. Now we may not like this freedom. Perhaps in our heart of hearts we would rather be guided and sustained by some infallible book of rules, or some infallible person. But God wants us to grow up, to learn to take intelligent moral decisions. And we only succeed in remaining childish if we cling to something which we think is infallible.

If we look back to our schooldays, we know that the teachers who did us the most good were neither the over-strict nor the over-lenient. It was those men or women who guided us and helped us, but who at the same time handed back to us a good deal of personal responsibility, to whom we were most indebted. That's naturally only a human example, but it serves to illustrate how the real and living God, while always ready to help and guide us by his Spirit, places in our hands a great deal of responsibility, so that we may grow up as his sons and daughters.

It is for this reason, I think, that Jesus asserted that "the Kingdom of God is within you". The Jews of his day were expecting a Messiah. They were looking for some leader to break in upon the pagan Roman conqueror with wrath and violence, with sword and fire. They were expecting God to rescue and vindicate his people in the sight of their enemies. It's not surprising that they didn't recognise Jesus as their rescuer, or appreciate his methods in founding a world-wide kingdom!

The situation is much the same today. People say, in effect, "If there is a God, why doesn't he show himself in power?" "Why doesn't he put a stop to evil?" "Why doesn't he remove sickness and want from the earth he's supposed to love?" Now we're not concerned with what we think God ought to do, but with what in fact he does do. And it would appear that God hands back to man much more responsibility than perhaps he bargains for. In theory and on paper, people are only too ready to see the fears and evils which afflict mankind removed. But how few are willing to act as God's agents, to work, at considerable personal cost, in the ceaseless battle against fear, disease, misery and want! "The Kingdom of God is within *you*," says Jesus, and it's really not the slightest good praying, "Thy Kingdom come, Thy Will be done, in earth as it is in heaven", unless we're prepared to work to make that prayer come true. The moment we're ready to do this, the moment we seriously enlist on the side of the Kingdom of God, we find that there is spiritual reinforcement readily available from God. The greatness of God is there all right. But it's an invisible greatness, perhaps as different from our pre-conceived ideas as the Jews' idea of the Messiah was from the actual Christ.

The Strength of God

Now I wrote, a moment ago, of the apparent weakness of God, but it is really a tremendous strength. You are at perfect liberty to defy God, to flout all his rules and make no attempt to co-operate with his purpose, and apparently there's nothing to stop you. But you and I only live because God has given us life. We use bodies and minds and faculties which we had no hand in designing. We live in a world which we had no part in creating, and after the death of the body we pass on to a stage about which we know very little. So, although it remains true that God will never force our hands or overpower our wills, yet this is his world in which we live and move and have our being. In that sense God is quite inescapable.

Now sometimes it appears to us that goodness is a weak thing. The men with a lust for power, the men with hard faces and tough consciences, appear to have the best time in this world, and the virtues of a Christ-like character appear to have little chance indeed against the tough, the violent and the evil. But in the end, whether it's in this world or the next, it will be plainly seen that goodness has a strange inner strength. What is more, goodness is permanent while evil is not. Goodness is part of the real and permanent because God is good, and although evil may survive in the mixed atmosphere of this world, sooner or later the game is up. There is no future in evil, only in good. People sometimes suddenly see this, even in this world. Peter saw it once when he saw in a flash the sheer goodness of Jesus, and cried out in terror, "Depart from me, for I am a sinful man, O Lord!" Saul saw it on the road to Damascus, when he suddenly realised that all his energies were being directed towards persecuting the real and good and permanent. He was travelling the wrong way in a one-way street! He was working against the very grain of the universe. And of course there have been thousands since those days who've seen, either suddenly or gradually, that God is in the long run undefeatable. It's a great day for any one of us when we perceive that this world, despite its evils and imperfections, is a good world, part of a good universe under the ultimate control of a good God.

The Purpose of God

Nevertheless, no one, as I understand the teaching of Christ, is ever going to be coerced or frightened into the Kingdom of God. The cross, the symbol of our faith and the very heart of its message, is not a sign of God's majesty and power conceived in earthly terms, but an unforgettable reminder of the lengths to which he will go to bring men to himself. It has evoked love and wonder and the willingness to serve in countless thousands. Few indeed remain unmoved once they have realised who it is who suffered. "Christ crucified" is, as Paul once said, both the power of God and the wisdom of God.

How true a picture, then, do we hold in our minds of the real greatness of God? It's easy to magnify human characteristics to the highest degree and imagine that such a conception somehow resembles the nature of God. Or we can imagine God as the mind infinitely greater than any of the marvels he creates and sustains. All that is awe-inspiring, and it's no bad thing to be awe-inspired, since we are probably very junior members of a complex universe! But size is not greatness, and awe is not love. And if we're to see the true greatness of God, and come to love and worship him, we must look again at Christ. Perhaps we shall see the unfailing patience, the unremitting love and the invincible purpose which is the true greatness of the living God.

GOD-BECOME-MAN The Purpose of God - 1

TO A great many people God remains a vast unknown Power. The more Science discovers of the complexities of the Universe the more impossible it seems to believe in a personal God. And yet, if ever God is to make himself known to us, he must, so to speak, speak our language, he must focus himself in a human being so that we may understand his character.

Christians believe that this planned focusing of God in a human being actually occurred nearly two thousand years ago, in the man called Jesus Christ. Those who knew him at the time took a little while to realise who he was. They admired his character, his teaching and his actions, but they didn't at first suspect that this was indeed God in human form. But when that mere handful of men and women did eventually realise who it was who had been living with them, they found that God, who had previously been unknowable, became knowable through Christ. The one who had always appeared to them so frightening in his power and holiness was seen to be their Father. They realised with a kind of dazed happiness that now that they believed in the focused God, they were reconciled with the purpose and will of God, and the spiritual resources of heaven flowed into their ordinary lives. More than thirty years after the death of Christ this extraordinary phenomenon was still happening. Here are parts of a letter that St. Paul wrote to Colossae, a town in Asia Minor:

> Now Christ is the visible expression of the invisible God. He existed before creation began, for it was through him that everything was made, whether spiritual or material, seen or unseen. Through him, and for him, also, were created power and dominion, ownership and authority. In fact, every single thing was created through, and for, him. He is both the first principle and the upholding principle of the whole scheme of creation. And now he is the head of the body which is the Church. Life from nothing began through him, and life from the dead began through him, and he is, therefore, justly called the Lord of all. It was in him that the full nature of God chose to live, and through him God planned to reconcile in his own person, as it were, everything on earth and everything in heaven by virtue of the sacrifice of the cross.
>
> And you yourselves, who were strangers to God, and, in fact, through the evil things you had done, his spiritual enemies, he has now reconciled through the death of his body on the cross, so that he might welcome you to his presence clean and pure, without blame or reproach.
>
> Be careful that nobody spoils your faith through intellectualism or high-sounding nonsense. Such stuff is at best founded on men's ideas of the nature of the world and disregards Christ! Yet it is in him that God gives a full and complete expression of himself (within the physical limits that he set himself in Christ). Moreover, your own completeness is

only realised in him, who is the authority over all authorities, and the supreme power over all powers.

As, therefore, God's picked representatives of the new humanity, purified and beloved of God himself, be merciful in action, kindly in heart, humble in mind. Accept life, and be most patient and tolerant with one another, always ready to forgive if you have a difference with anyone. Forgive as freely as Christ has forgiven you. And, above everything else, be truly loving, for love is the golden chain of all the virtues.

(Coloss. 1: *15–22*, 2: *8–10*, 3: *12–14*)

THE EXPRESSION OF GOD   The Purpose of God – 2

WE HAVE spoken of the necessity for accepting what I called the "focused God", or God-become-man, whom we know as Jesus Christ, if we are to know God at all. For unless we accept what I believe was God's deliberate action, we may have our guesses and our intuitions and our bright ideas, but we do not in fact know God as a person or as a living power within ourselves. We read from one of the earliest of the New Testament writings where St. Paul was writing to the young Church of Colossae. Read now some words written by St. John in the fourth Gospel, probably some thirty years later. You will remember in your Authorised Version of the Bible that the opening words are these:

> In the beginning was the Word, and the Word was with God, and the Word was God.

Unless you happen to be an instructed Christian already, I am pretty sure that those words sound almost incomprehensible. Quite probably they were *not* incomprehensible to the people for whom St. John was writing, since the idea of a divine Word, or "Logos" as it is in the Greek, was quite common among the philosophically-minded of the Jews at that time. But I am pretty certain that it is most *uncommon* in the minds of most English-speaking people of today. It simply sounds more or less like a religious technical term and probably means very little. So in my own translation I have translated the word "Logos" by the words "express" and "expression", for I'm pretty certain that we all realise that without words we are not able to express ourselves properly, and that the words that a person speaks are the expression of his thoughts. So in that sense God expressed himself in Jesus Christ. For in order to make himself known to us men, he had to express himself in human terms. With these thoughts in mind, read now the familiar words of the opening of St. John's Gospel, translated in what are unfamiliar words. You may find, indeed I hope you will find, that they begin to make fresh sense to you in this changed form:

> At the beginning God expressed himself. That personal expression, that word, was with God and

was God, and he existed with God from the beginning. All creation took place through him, and none took place without him. In him appeared life and this life was the light of mankind. The light still shines in the darkness, and the darkness has never put it out.

A man called John was sent by God as a witness to the light, so that any man who heard his testimony might believe in the light. This man was not himself the light: he was sent simply as a personal witness to that light.

That was the true light which shines on every man as he comes into the world. He came into the world – the world he had created – and the world failed to recognise him. He came into his own creation, and his own people would not accept him. Yet wherever men did accept him he gave them the power to become sons of God. These were the men who truly believed in him, and their birth depended not on the course of nature nor on any impulse or plan of man, but on God.

So the word of God became a human being and lived among us. We saw his splendour (the splendour as of a father's only son), full of grace and truth. Indeed, every one of us has shared in his riches – there is a grace in our lives because of his grace. For while the Law was given by Moses, love and truth came through Jesus Christ. It is true that no one has ever seen God at any time. Yet the divine and only Son, who lives in the closest intimacy with the Father, has made him known.

(John 1: *1–18*)

THE CHARACTER OF JESUS The Purpose of God – 3

IF WE are Christians, that is, if we have accepted the basic fact that Jesus Christ was God expressed in a human being, and have begun to live our lives according to what he taught, it becomes very important to study the four Gospels. We want to see as clearly as we possibly can the sort of character that Jesus Christ revealed. For we are seeing, not indeed the whole of God, but an authentic and reliable expression of God, as far as he could be expressed in a human being.

Now we might have expected such a perfect being to go around underlining people's sins and generally making them feel guilty and afraid. It is true that Christ used the most scathing language towards religious hypocrites and others who needed to be shocked out of their complacency. But in general we seldom find him calling ordinary people sinners. His method appears to have been to call to the real man, which exists in every one of us, however feeble and blind it may have become, to follow him.

Read now how he called Levi, a most unlikely follower – a man who had built up a comfortable racket in the tax-collecting line. And mark Levi's quite astonishing response:

> Jesus left there and as he passed on he saw Levi the son of Alphaeus sitting at his desk in the tax-collector's office, and he said to him, "Follow me!"

Levi got up and followed him. Later, when Jesus was sitting at dinner in Levi's house, a large number of tax-collectors and disreputable folk came in and joined him and his disciples. For there were many such people among his followers. When the Scribes and Pharisees saw him eating in the company of tax-collectors and outsiders, they remarked to his disciples.

"Why does he eat with tax-collectors and sinners?"

When Jesus heard this, he said to them,

"It is not the fit and flourishing who need the doctor, but those who are ill. I did not come to invite the 'righteous', but the 'sinners'."

(Mark 2: *14–17*)

We notice that his purpose is not to collect those who think themselves good. There was something in these 'sinners' and 'outsiders', as the world called them, which responded to the call of Christ.

Again, when he called Zacchaeus, he saw beyond the façade, the hard face and the mean ways. He saw the man Zacchaeus longed to be – good and generous and kind.

Then he went into Jericho and was making his way through it. And here we find a wealthy man called Zacchaeus, a chief collector of taxes, wanting to see what sort of person Jesus was. But the crowd prevented him from doing so, for he was very short. So he ran ahead and climbed up into a sycamore tree to get a view of Jesus as he was heading that way. When Jesus reached the spot, he looked up and saw the man and said,

"Zacchaeus, hurry up and come down, I must be your guest today."

So Zacchaeus hurriedly climbed down and gladly welcomed him. But the bystanders muttered their disapproval saying, "Now he has gone to stay with a real sinner."

But Zacchaeus himself stopped and said to the Lord,

"Look, sir, I will give half my property to the poor. And if I have swindled anybody out of anything I will pay him back four times as much."

Jesus said to him,

"Salvation has come to this house today. Zacchaeus is a descendant of Abraham and it was the lost that the Son of Man came to seek – and to save."

(Luke 19: *1–10*)

JESUS HEALING The Purpose of God – 4

IF WE accept the core and centre of the Christian faith, which means believing that Jesus Christ was truly God walking this earth in human form, we are naturally extremely interested to see, not only what kind of person he was, but what kind of things he did. Most of his actions fall under the heading of either healing, that is restoring the true order of physical, mental or spiritual life, as God meant it to be; or teaching, in which he told people how life was meant to be lived. Here is an account from the fifth chapter of St. Mark's Gospel, where Christ heals two people, one very young and one getting on in years. Notice that he, the source of all life, is able to restore health in the most apparently hopeless cases. Read it now in modern English, as though you hadn't heard the story before, and remember that the one who does this healing is the one whom we worship as God.

When Jesus had crossed again in the boat to the other side of the lake, a great crowd collected around him as he stood on the shore. Then came a man called Jairus, one of the synagogue presidents. And when he saw Jesus, he knelt before him, pleading for his help.
"My little girl is dying," he said. "Will you come and put your hands on her – then she will get better and live." Jesus went off with him, followed by a large crowd jostling at his elbow. Among them was a woman who had had a haemorrhage for twelve years and who had gone through a great deal at the hands of many doctors, spending all her money in the process. She had derived no benefit from them but, on the contrary, was getting worse. This woman had heard about Jesus and came up behind him under cover of the crowd, and touched his cloak.
"For if I can only touch his clothes", she kept saying, "I shall be all right."
The haemorrhage stopped immediately, and she knew in herself that she was cured of her trouble. At once Jesus knew intuitively that power had gone out of him, and he turned round in the middle of the crowd and said,
"Who touched my clothes?"

His disciples replied,

"You can see this crowd jostling you. How can you ask, 'Who touched me?'"

But he looked all round at their faces to see who had done so. Then the woman, scared and shaking all over because she knew that she was the one to whom this thing had happened, came and flung herself before him and told him the whole story. But he said to her,

"Daughter, it is your faith that has healed you. Go home in peace, and be free from your trouble."

While he was still speaking, messengers arrived from the synagogue president's house, saying,

"Your daughter is dead – there is no need to bother the Master any further."

But when Jesus heard this, he said,

"Now don't be afraid, just go on believing!"

Then he allowed no one to follow him except Peter and James and John, James's brother. They arrived at the president's house and Jesus noticed the hubbub and all the weeping and wailing, and as he went in, he said to the people in the house, "Why are you making such a noise with your crying? The child is not dead; she is fast asleep."

They greeted this with a scornful laugh. But Jesus turned them all out, and taking only the father and mother and his own companions with him, went into the room where the child was. Then he took the little girl's hand and said to her in Aramaic,

"Little girl, I tell you to get up!"

At once she jumped to her feet and walked round the room, for she was twelve years old. This sight sent the others nearly out of their minds with joy.

But Jesus gave them strict instructions not to let anyone know what had happened – and ordered food to be given to the little girl.

(Mark 5: *21–43*)

JESUS TEACHING The Purpose of God – 5

WE HAVE just read a story, a true story, of the sort of healing work which God-become-man, whom we call Jesus Christ, did during his earthly life. Now I want to quote a sample of his teaching. But before I do that, I feel I must remind you how very revolutionary most of this teaching is. In fact it's quite often the direct opposite of what most people think. The example I have chosen comes from what we all know as the Sermon on the Mount, from what we probably knew as children as "The Beatitudes". Again, before we read these famous words in modern English, I must remind you that the word translated "Blessed" in the Authorised Version is very nearly the equivalent of our modern word "happy". So that Jesus is in effect giving us a "recipe for happiness". Then, so as to make the revolutionary character of his recipe more apparent, I will quote first a little version of my own of what most non-Christian people think. They think:

Happy are the "pushers": for they get on in the the world.

Happy are the hard-boiled: for they never let life hurt them.

Happy are they who complain: for they get their own way in the end.

Happy are the blasé: for they never worry over their sins.

Happy are the slave-drivers: for they get results.

Happy are the knowledgeable men of the world: for they know their way around.

Happy are the trouble-makers: for they make people take notice of them."

But Jesus Christ said:

How happy are the humble-minded, for the Kingdom of Heaven is theirs!

How happy are those who know what sorrow means, for they will be given courage and comfort!

Happy are those who claim nothing, for the whole earth will belong to them!

Happy are those who are hungry and thirsty for goodness, for they will be fully satisfied!

Happy are the merciful, for they will have mercy shown to them!

Happy are the utterly sincere, for they will see God!

Happy are those who make peace, for they will be known as sons of God! (Matthew 4: *3–10*)

You could hardly have a more complete reversal of worldly values than that, could you? Most people are trying the first recipe that I mentioned, and the result is a world full of unhappiness, greed, cruelty and selfishness. The method that Jesus Christ recommends not only makes for much more happiness all round, but, strangely, enough, means real security, security of soul. Listen to these further words of his:

> Everyone then who hears these words of mine and puts them into practice is like a sensible man who built his house on the rock. Down came the rain and up came the floods, while the winds blew and roared upon that house – and it did not fall because its foundations were on the rock.
> And everyone who hears these words of mine and does not follow them can be compared with a foolish man who built his house on the sand. Down came the rain and up came the floods, while the winds blew and battered that house till it collapsed and fell with a great crash.
>
> (Matthew 7: *24-27*)

I think – no, I am sure – that those who seriously follow the way of living which Jesus recommended will find that his words are absolutely true. That way lies happiness. They may sound idealistic and fanciful, but if you try to live by them, you will find they are down-to-earth and practical. Your life becomes like a house built upon a rock.

FORGIVENESS AND FORGIVINGNESS
The Purpose of God – 6

ONE OF the most astonishing things that Jesus Christ ever said was that men cannot hope to be forgiven by God unless they are prepared to forgive the people who offend or hurt them. I sometimes think this very searching truth has been soft-pedalled, but it's very evident in the Gospels. Every time we say the Lord's Prayer we say, "Forgive us our trespasses as we forgive them that trespass against us", and Jesus added:

"For if you forgive other people their failures your Heavenly Father will also forgive you: but if you will not forgive other people neither will your Heavenly Father forgive your failures. "
(Matthew 6: *14–15*)

If we could only see for a moment how much God is prepared to forgive us, and how comparatively little we are prepared to forgive other people, we might have a good laugh at ourselves, which would do us a lot of good, as well as help us to know much more of what being at peace with God means. Jesus tried to bring this home to his hearers by a vivid little story.

Then Peter approached him with the question, "Master, how many times can my brother wrong me and I must forgive him? Would seven times be enough?"
"No," replied Jesus, "not seven times, but seventy times seven. For the Kingdom of Heaven is like a king who decided to settle his accounts with his servants. When he had started calling in his accounts, a man was brought to him who owed him millions of pounds. And when it was plain that he had no means of repaying the debt, his master gave orders for him to be sold as a slave, and his wife and children and all his possessions as well, and the money to be paid over. At this the servant fell on his knees before his master. 'Oh, be patient with

me!' he cried, 'and I will pay you back every penny!' Then his master was moved with pity for him, set him free and cancelled his debt.

"But when this same servant had left his master's presence, he found one of his fellow-servants who owed him a few shillings. He grabbed him and seized him by the throat, crying, 'Pay up what you owe me!' At this his fellow-servant fell down at his feet, and implored him, 'Oh, be patient with me, and I will pay you back!' But he refused and went out and had him put in prison until he should repay the debt.

"When the other fellow-servants saw what had happened, they were horrified and went and told their master the whole incident. Then his master called him in.

"'You wicked servant!' he said. 'Didn't I cancel all that debt when you begged me to do so? Oughtn't you to have taken pity on your fellow-servant as I, your master, took pity on you? And his master in anger handed him over to the gaolers till he should repay the whole debt. This is how my Heavenly Father will treat you unless you each forgive your brother from your heart."

(Matthew 18: *21–35*)

Jesus obviously regarded it as very important indeed for us to forgive each other fully and freely. Unless we do that our service to God, or our giving to God, has no value at all. Moreover, Jesus emphasises the need to forgive quickly while we have the chance. Some of us may know what it is to have refused to forgive while we had the opportunity, and then we have found that bearing a grudge against somebody perhaps for months or years becomes a miserable prison to our souls. Hence these words of Christ:

> "So that if, while you are offering your gift at the altar, you should remember that your brother has something against you, you must leave your gift there before the altar and go away. Make your peace with your brother first, then come and offer your gift. Come to terms quickly with your opponent while you have the chance, or else he may hand you over to the judge and the judge in turn hand you over to the officer of the court and you will be thrown into prison. Believe me, you will never get out again till you have paid out your last farthing."
> (Matthew 5: *23–26*)

RELIGION AND LIFE The Purpose of God – 7

WE HAVE been speaking of the necessity of forgiving each other if we want to be forgiven by God. And I quoted the words of Christ to show that the two are very closely linked together. I'm not sure that we all really believe this, especially if we are religious people. Somehow or other we expect to be able to pray to God and make our gifts to God, and to keep that in a quite separate department from our relationship with other people. Believe me, Jesus Christ would never have allowed that for a moment. That is why quite the most frightening thing to me about the

Gospels is that the religious people of his day were his deadly enemies, and called forth his most shattering denunciation. You see, they had divorced, or attempted to divorce, religion and ordinary human relationships, and that is a thing Jesus would never stand for! Read this unforgettable little story:

"Two men went up to the Temple to pray, one was a Pharisee, the other was a tax-collector. The Pharisee stood and prayed like this with himself: 'O God, I do thank thee that I am not like the rest of mankind, greedy, dishonest, impure, or even like that tax-collector over there. I fast twice every week; I give away a tenth-part of all my income.' But the tax-collector stood in a distant corner, scarcely daring to look up to Heaven, and with a gesture of despair, said, 'God, have mercy on a sinner like me.' I assure you that he was the man who went home justified in God's sight rather than the other one." (Luke 18: *10-14*)

That is a story that Jesus told, but here is an actual incident which illustrates the point very well:

Then one of the Pharisees asked Jesus to a meal with him. When Jesus came into the house, he took his place at the table and a woman, known in the town as a bad woman, found out that Jesus was there and brought an alabaster flask of perfume and stood behind him crying, letting her tears fall on his feet and then drying them with her hair. Then she kissed them and anointed them with the perfume. When the Pharisee who had invited him saw this, he said to himself, "If this man were really a prophet, he would know who this woman is and what sort of a person is touching him. He would have realised that she is a bad woman."

Then Jesus spoke to him,

"Simon, there is something I want to say to you."

"Very well, Master," he returned, "say it."

"Once upon a time there were two men in debt to the same money-lender. One owed him fifty pounds and the other five. And since they were both unable to pay, he generously cancelled both their debts. Now, which one of them do you suppose will love him more?"

"Well," returned Simon, "I suppose it will be the one who has been more generously treated."

"Exactly," replied Jesus, and then turning to the woman, he said to Simon,

"You can see this woman? I came into your house but you provided no water to wash my feet. But she has washed my feet with her tears and dried them with her hair. There was no warmth in your greeting, but she, from the moment I came in, has not stopped covering my feet with kisses. You gave me no oil for my head, but she has put perfume on my feet. That is why I tell you, Simon, that her sins, many as they are, are forgiven; for she has shown me so much love. But the man who has little to be forgiven has only a little love to give."

(Luke 7: *36–47*)

POWER OVER DEATH　　　The Purpose of God – 8

SUCH, THEN, were the actions of Jesus Christ, who was God in human form. In the face of sickness he restored God's true order of health; in the face of ignorance and hypocrisy he proclaimed truth; he told men how to live. Consider now what he did when he was confronted by man's last enemy – death. Lazarus, brother of Martha and Mary, had died in the village of Bethany, and an urgent message was sent to Jesus just before he died. But although Jesus loved the three of them very dearly, he didn't hurry to the scene – not that he was unsympathetic, as you will see, but because he wanted them all to realise that he who was the Son of God had power even over death.

When Jesus arrived, he found that Lazarus had already been in the grave four days. Now Bethany is quite near Jerusalem, rather less than two miles away, and a good many of the Jews had come out to see Martha and Mary to offer them sympathy over their brother's death. When Martha heard that Jesus was on his way, she went out and met him, while Mary stayed in the house.

"If only you had been here, Lord," said Martha, "my brother would never have died. And I know that, even now, God will give you whatever you ask from him."

"Your brother will rise again," Jesus replied to her.

"I know," said Martha, "that he will rise again in the resurrection at the last day."

"I myself am the resurrection and the life," Jesus told her. "The man who believes in me will live even though he dies, and anyone who is alive and believes in me will never die at all. Can you believe that?"

"Yes, Lord," replied Martha. "I do believe that

you are Christ, the Son of God, the one who was to come into the world."

Saying this, she went away and called Mary her sister, whispering "The Master's here and is asking for you." When Mary heard this she sprang to her feet and went to him. Now Jesus had not yet arrived at the village itself, but was still where Martha had met him. So when the Jews who had been condoling with Mary in the house saw her get up quickly, they followed her, imagining that she was going off to the grave to weep there.

When Mary met Jesus, she looked at him and then fell down at his feet. "If only you had been here, Lord," she said, "my brother would never have died."

When Jesus saw Mary weep and noticed the tears of the Jews who came with her, he was deeply moved and visibly distressed.

"Where have you put him?" he asked.

"Lord, come and see," they replied, and at this Jesus himself wept.

"Look how much he loved him!" remarked the Jews, though some of them asked, "Could he not have kept this man from dying if he could open that blind man's eyes?"

Jesus was again deeply moved at these words, and went on to the grave. It was a cave, and a stone lay in front of it.

"Take away the stone," said Jesus.

"But Lord," said Martha, the dead man's sister, "he has been dead four days. By this time he will be decaying. . . ."

"Did I not tell you," replied Jesus, "that, if you believed, you would see the wonder of what God can do?"

Then they took the stone away and Jesus raised his eyes and said, "Father, I thank you that you have heard me. I know that you always hear me but I have said this for the sake of these people standing here so that they may believe that you have sent me."

And when he had said this, he called out in a loud voice, "Lazarus, come out!"

And the dead man came out, his hands and feet bound with grave-clothes and his face muffled with a handkerchief.

"Now unbind him," Jesus told them, "and let him go home."

(John 11: *17–44*)

CHRIST DIED FOR US The Purpose of God – 9

AS THE earthly life of Jesus drew towards its end, he seems to have regarded his own death as inevitable. The forces of evil, cruelty, greed for power, hypocrisy and all the rest conspired together to get him crucified on a trumped-up charge. It mystified and even scared the disciples when he went for the last time to Jerusalem to face certain death. "He walked ahead," we read, "and they followed, with fear in their hearts."

What puzzled and frightened the early disciples may, if we think about it seriously, also puzzle and frighten us. There is a real horror in watching

God-become-man allowing the forces of evil to move in upon him with deadly intent. If ever there was a case for divine intervention, we may feel, this is it; and we may well be puzzled as to why the natural sequence of evil events went remorselessly on and the Son of God was brutally flogged and then crucified.

He himself said remarkably little about his own death. He spoke of "giving his life a ransom for many": at the Last Supper he spoke of his body being broken and his blood shed "for the remission of sins": and he spoke briefly of his own death as a bitter necessity – "for thus it must be".

It was only after Christ's death that men began to realise the significance of the action. This is how Paul interpreted it about twenty-five years afterwards:

> And we can see that it was while we were powerless to help ourselves that Christ died for sinful men. In human experience it is a rare thing for one man to give his life for another, even if the latter be a good man, though there have been a few who have had the courage to do it. Yet the proof of God's amazing love is this: that it was *while we were sinners* that Christ died for us. Moreover, if he did that for us while we were sinners, now that we are men justified by the shedding of his blood, what reason have we to fear the wrath of God? If, while we were his enemies, Christ reconciled us to God by *dying for us*, surely now that we are reconciled we may be perfectly certain of our salvation through His *living in us*. Nor, I am sure, is this a matter of bare salvation – we may hold our heads high in the light

of God's love because of the reconciliation which Christ has made.

Now what is our response to be? Shall we sin to our heart's content and see how far we can exploit the grace of God? What a ghastly thought! We, who have died to sin – how could we live in sin a moment longer? Have you forgotten that all of us who were baptised into Jesus Christ were, by that very action, sharing in his death? We were dead and buried with him in baptism, so that, just as he was raised from the dead by that splendid revelation of the Father's power, so we too might rise to life on a new plane altogether. If we have, as it were, shared his death, let us rise and live our new lives with him! Let us never forget that our old selves died with him on the cross that the tyranny of sin over us might be broken – for a dead man can safely be said to be immune to the power of sin. And if we were dead men with him we can believe that we shall also be men newly alive with him. We can be sure that the risen Christ never dies again – death's power to touch him is finished. He died, because of sin, once: he lives for God for ever. In the same way look upon yourselves as dead to the appeal and power of sin but alive and sensitive to the call of God through Jesus Christ our Lord. (Romans 5: *6*–6: *11*)

JUSTIFIED BY FAITH　　　The Purpose of God – 10

WE HAVE been thinking of the mystery of Christ's act of reconciliation, his own death on the cross. Without expounding theories of atonement, we can certainly say this – that it means a real revolution in a man's thinking when he realises that what he could never do has already been done. He need no longer try and "put up a case" or try to justify himself before God – which is hopeless anyway. All he has to do, according to the Gospel of the New Testament, is to transfer his central confidence in his own goodness and abilities to Christ who is the son of God and also representative man. That is what the New Testament writers mean by "faith". In Christ he will find he can begin to know God, and begin to share that timeless quality of living which the New Testament calls "eternal life". Here we see a good religious man face to face with Jesus Christ:

> One night Nicodemus, a leading Jew and Pharisee, came to see Jesus.
> "Master," he began, "we realise that you are a teacher who has come from God. Obviously no one could show the signs that you show unless God were with him."
> "Believe me," returned Jesus, "a man cannot even see the kingdom of God without being born again."
> "And how can a man who's getting old possibly be born?" replied Nicodemus. "How can he go back into his mother's womb and be born a second time?"
> "I assure you," said Jesus, "that unless a man is born from water and from spirit he cannot enter the kingdom of God. Flesh gives birth to flesh and spirit gives birth to spirit: you must not be surprised that I told you that all of you must be born again. The wind blows where it likes, you can hear the

sound of it but you have no idea where it comes from and where it goes. Nor can you tell how a man is born by the wind of the Spirit."

"How on earth can things like this happen?" replied Nicodemus.

"So you are a teacher of Israel," said Jesus, "and you do not recognise such things? I assure you that we are talking about something we really know and we are witnessing to something we have actually observed, yet men like you will not accept our evidence. Yet if I have spoken to you about things which happen on this earth and you will not believe me, what chance is there that you will believe me if I tell you about what happens in Heaven? No one has ever been up to Heaven except the Son of Man who came down from Heaven. The Son of Man must be lifted above the heads of men – as Moses lifted up that serpent in the desert – so that any man who believes in him may have eternal life. For God loved the world so much that he gave his only Son, so that everyone who believes in him should not be lost, but should have eternal life. You must understand that God has not sent his son into the world to pass sentence upon it, but to save it – through him. Any man who believes in him is not judged at all. It is the one who will not believe who stands already condemned, because he will not believe in the character of God's only Son. This *is* the judgement – that light has entered the world and men have preferred darkness to light because their deeds are evil. Anybody who does wrong hates the light and keeps away from it, for fear his deeds may be exposed. But anybody who is living by the truth will come to the light to make it plain that all he has done has been done through God."

(John 3: *1–21*)

HE WALKED THROUGH DEATH

The Purpose of God – 11

WE HAVE been thinking of the importance of the mysterious death of Christ. But death was not the end for the Man who was also God. He, so to speak, walked right through death, as he said he would, and came back to show himself, not once, but again and again, to his astonished followers. They were sunk in gloom and despondency; they were in no mood for tricks or swindles or hallucinations. Read this well-known story of the two who went for a walk on that first Easter Sunday:

> Then on the same day we find two of them going off to Emmaus, a village about seven miles from Jerusalem. As they went they were deep in conversation about everything that had happened. While they were absorbed in their serious talk and discussion, Jesus himself approached and walked along with them, but something prevented them from recognising him. Then he spoke to them,
> "What is all this discussion that you are having on your walk?"
> They stopped, their faces drawn with misery, and the one called Cleopas replied,
> "You must be the only stranger in Jerusalem who hasn't heard all the things that have happened there recently!"
> "What things?" asked Jesus.
> "Oh, all about Jesus, from Nazareth. There was a

man – a prophet strong in what he did and what he said, in God's eyes as well as the people's. Haven't you heard how our chief priests and rulers handed him over for execution, and had him crucified? But we were hoping he was the one who was to come and set Israel free. . . .

"Yes, and as if that were not enough, it's getting on for three days since all this happened; and some of our womenfolk have disturbed us profoundly. They went to the tomb at dawn, and then when they couldn't find his body they said that they had had a vision of angels who said that he was alive. Some of our people went straight off to the tomb and found things just as the women had described them – but they didn't see *him*!"

Then he himself spoke to them,

"Aren't you failing to understand, and slow to believe in all the things that the prophets have said? Was it not inevitable that Christ should suffer like that and so find his glory?"

Then, beginning with Moses and all the prophets, he explained to them everything in the scriptures that referred to himself.

They were by now approaching the village to which they were going. He gave the impression that he meant to go on further, but they stopped him with the words,

"Do stay with us. It is nearly evening and soon the day will be over."

So he went indoors to stay with them. Then it happened! While he was sitting at table with them he took the loaf, gave thanks, broke it and passed it to them. Their eyes opened wide and they knew him! But he vanished from their sight. Then they said to each other,

"Weren't our hearts glowing while he was with us on the road, and when he made the scriptures so plain to us?"

And they got to their feet without delay and turned back to Jerusalem. There they found the eleven and their friends all together, full of the news —

"The Lord is really risen – he has appeared to Simon now!" Then they told the story of their walk, and how they recognised him when he broke the loaf. (Mark 27: *13–35*)

THE DIVINE HELPER The Purpose of God – 12

AFTER JESUS had risen from the dead he showed himself on a good many occasions to those who believed in him. As far as we know, this process of appearing to them, teaching them, and then withdrawing himself again, went on for about six weeks after the actual resurrection. We can, I think, infer that one of the reasons for this period of appearance and disappearance was to accustom them to the idea that, although they would have to get on without his visible presence, yet by his Spirit, which he promised he would send, he would truly always be with them. Just before his death, according to St. John's record, he told them about the Spirit of truth, the divine helper, who would come to them. It seems that they must have forgotten this promise, at any rate temporarily, after what seemed to them the ultimate disaster – his death upon the cross. But of course they remembered this promise later, and St. John records these words of Christ:

. . . "None of you asks me 'Where are you going?' That is because you are so distressed at what I have told you. Yet I am telling you the simple truth when I assure you that it is a good thing for you that I should go away. For if I did not go away, the divine helper would not come to you. But if I go, then I will send him to you. When he comes, he will convince the world of the meaning of sin, true goodness and judgement. He will expose their sin because they do not believe in me; he will reveal true goodness for I am going away to the Father and you will see me no longer; and he will show them the meaning of judgement, for the spirit which rules this world will have been judged.

"I have much more to tell you but you cannot bear it now. Yet when that one I have spoken to you about comes – the Spirit of truth – he will guide you into everything that is true.

. . ."In a little while you will not see me any longer, and again, in a little while you will see me.

. . . "I have been speaking to you in parables – but the time is coming to give up parables and tell you plainly about the Father. When that time comes you will make your requests to him in my name, for I need make no promise to plead to the Father for you, for the Father himself loves you, because you have loved me and have believed that I came from God. Yes, I did come from the Father and I came into the world. Now I leave the world behind and return to the Father."

"Now you are speaking plainly," cried the

disciples, "and are not using parables. Now we know that everything is known to you – no more questions are needed. This makes us sure that you did come from God."

"So you believe in me now?" replied Jesus. "The time is coming, indeed, it has already come, when you will be scattered, every one of you going home and leaving me alone. Yet I am not really alone, for the Father is with me. I have told you all this so that you may find your peace in me. You will find trouble in the world – but, never lose heart, I have conquered the world!" (John 16: *6–33*)

THE SPIRIT AT WORK The Purpose of God – 13

AFTER JESUS CHRIST had left this earth he sent, as he promised, his own Spirit, to guide, inspire and support his early followers. The well-known story in the second chapter of the Acts of the Apostles tells of the sudden dramatic giving of that dynamic Spirit to the assembled disciples on the day of Pentecost. That particularly impressive pouring out of the Spirit into human life was never, as far as we know, repeated. But the New Testament letters positively bristle with references to that same Spirit coming into human lives in transforming power. Indeed this is the true wonder of the Christian faith – that where men are ready to receive him the very Spirit of God does come into human lives and changes their direction, their quality and their power. St. Paul, for example, writing nearly a quarter of a century after Pentecost, tells the Galatians that this is what he has observed:

> The Spirit produces in human life fruits such as these: love, joy, peace, patience, kindness, generosity, fidelity, tolerance and self-control.
> (Gal. 5: *22-3*)

And then at about the same time, he says:

> Men have different gifts, but it is the same Spirit who gives them. There are different ways of serving God, but it is the same Lord who is served. God works through different men in different ways. But it is the same God who achieves his purposes through them all. Each man is given his gift by the Spirit that he may use it for the common good. One man's gift by the Spirit is to speak with wisdom, another's to speak with knowledge. The same Spirit gives to another man faith, to another the ability to heal, to another the power to do great deeds. The same Spirit gives to another man the gift of preaching the word of God, to another the ability to discriminate in spiritual matters, to another speech in different tongues and to yet another the power to interpret the tongues. Behind all these gifts is the operation of the same Spirit, who distributes to each individual man, as he wills.
> (I Cor. 12: *4-11*)

Again, writing his second letter to Timothy, he says:

> For God has not given us a spirit of fear, but the Spirit of power and love and a sound mind.
> (II Timothy 1: *6*)

Again, when he writes to the Romans, he says:

> You cannot, indeed, be a Christian at all unless you have something of his Spirit in you. Now if Christ does live within you his presence means that your sinful nature is dead, but your spirit becomes alive because of the righteousness he brings with him I said that our nature is "dead" in the presence of Christ, and so it is, because of its sin. Nevertheless, once the Spirit that raised Jesus from the dead lives within you he will, by that same Spirit, bring to your whole being new strength and vitality. . . . All who follow the leading of God's Spirit are God's own sons. . . . The Spirit himself endorses our inward conviction that we really are the children of God.
> (Romans 8: *9-16*)

TRANSFORMED FROM WITHIN
The Purpose of God – 14

UP TO the time of the coming of the Christian faith, religion had been almost entirely a matter of obeying the laws of an "external" God. It is true that in the Old Testament there are hints and promises of God putting his own Spirit inside men's personalities, but this did not come true until the Christian Church came into being. The old way of looking at things, as St. Paul says again and again, was a matter of obedience to the divine Law. The new thing which Christ brought into being was that God himself, by his

Spirit, was entering into men's hearts, and transforming them *from inside*. St. Paul looks upon this as God's great "secret", which he and his fellow-Christians were now privileged to understand. Thus:

> I am a minister of the Church by divine commission, a commission granted to me for your benefit and for a special purpose: that I might fully declare God's Word – that sacred mystery which up till now has been hidden in every age and in every generation, but which is now as clear as daylight to those who love God. They are those to whom God has planned to give a vision of the full wonder and splendour of his secret plan for the sons of men. And this secret is simply this: Christ *in you*! Yes, Christ *in you* bringing with him the hope of all the glorious things to come.
> (Coloss. 1: *25-27*)

Then again, writing to the Ephesians in the same year, he tells the new converts his prayer for them:

> That God, the God of our Lord Jesus Christ and the all-glorious Father will give you spiritual wisdom and the insight to know more of him: that you may receive that inner illumination of the spirit which will make you realise how great is the hope to which he is calling you – the magnificence and splendour of the inheritance promised to Christians – and how tremendous is the power available to us who believe in God. That power is the same divine energy which was demonstrated in Christ when he raised him from the dead.
> (Ephes. 1: *17-20*)

St. John puts the same thing – the idea that God is

powerfully at work within the personality of the Christian – into different words. In his first letter he says:

> Consider the incredible love that the Father has shown us in allowing us to be called "children of God" – and that is not just what we are called, but what we *are*. Our heredity on the God-ward side is no mere figure of speech. . . . Oh, dear children of mine, have you realised it? Here and now we *are* God's children. . . .
> The man who is really God's son does not practise sin, for God's nature is in him, for good, and such a heredity is incapable of sin.
> Everyone who acknowledges that Jesus is the Son of God finds that God lives in him, and he lives in God. So have we come to know and trust the love God has for us. God *is* love, and the man whose life is lived in love does, in fact, live in God, and God does, in fact, live in him.
>
> (I John 3: *1–9*, 4: *15–16*)

LIFE IN THE SPIRIT   The Purpose of God – 15

THE HEART of the Christian faith is simple but quite revolutionary. It is that a man's relations with God are no longer a matter of obedience to an "external" God, but a willingness to be led by God's own Spirit within him. Reconciliation with God is made possible by Christ, who is God as well as man, for, to use St. Paul's words, "God was in Christ reconciling the world unto himself". And it is by believing in a living Spirit within us that we can know the friendship of God and can experience his power and love actually operating within ourselves. But, for some reason or other, human nature has a tendency to slip backwards, and then religion becomes once more a matter of rules and regulations, instead of fellowship with the living Christ. This happened to the Christians in Galatia, and St. Paul had to write to them quite firmly:

O you dear idiots of Galatia, who saw Jesus Christ the crucified so plainly, who has been casting a spell over you? I will ask you one simple question: did you receive the Spirit by trying to keep the Law or by believing the message of the gospel? Surely you can't be so idiotic as to think that a man begins his spiritual life in the Spirit and then completes it by reverting to outward observances? Has all your painful experience brought you nowhere? I simply cannot believe it of you! Does God, who gives you his Spirit and works miracles among you, do these things because you have obeyed the Law or because you have believed the gospel? Ask yourselves that.

For now that you have faith in Christ Jesus you are all sons of God. All of you who were baptised "into" Christ have put on the family likeness of Christ. Gone is the distinction between Jew and Greek, slave and free man, male and female – you are all one in Christ Jesus!

At one time when you had no knowledge of God, you were under the authority of gods who had no real existence. But now that you have come to know God, or rather, are known by him, how can you revert to dead and sterile principles and consent to be under their power all over again? Your religion is beginning to be a matter of observing certain days or months or years. Frankly, you stagger me; you make me wonder if all my efforts over you have been wasted.

Plant your feet firmly within the freedom that Christ has won for us, and do not let yourselves be caught again in the shackles of slavery. . . . If you try to be justified by the Law you automatically cut yourselves off from the power of Christ, you put yourself outside the range of his grace. For it is *by faith* that we await in his Spirit the righteousness we hope to see.

Here is my advice. Live your whole life in the Spirit and you will not satisfy the desires of your lower nature.

(Gal. 3: *1-28*, 4: *8-11*, 5: *1-16*)

A NEW SPIRIT   The Purpose of God – 16

I HAVE already referred, more than once, to the revolutionary character of the Christian faith, and to how it means being transformed from within, rather than merely obeying external rules. St. Paul was the great pioneer of this, the heart of the Gospel, and his bitter enemies, almost everywhere he went, were those who had reduced religion to a matter of rules and regulations. The same thing, of course, had happened to his Lord and Master, Jesus Christ, a quarter of a century before. The Scribes and Pharisees were the implacable enemies of the Son of God himself. Because he insisted that the rule of God, or Kingdom of God, began inside a man, in his heart, he appeared to them to be flouting all their outward laws and principles. But Jesus Christ, and St. Paul, were right, of course, and the formalists and legalists were wrong. For men are not really changed at heart by outward regulation, but only when a new Spirit comes into their lives. St. Paul sees this as a vast and patient work of reconciliation whereby the infinite love of God seeks to bring men into harmony with himself. Read, for example, these words:

> For if a man is in Christ he becomes a new person altogether – the past is finished and gone, everything has become fresh and new. All this is God's doing, for he has reconciled us to himself through Jesus Christ; and he has made us agents of the reconciliation. God was in Christ personally reconciling the world to himself – not counting their sins against them – and has commissioned us with the message of reconciliation. We are now Christ's ambassadors, as though God were appealing direct to you through us. As his personal representatives we say, "Make your peace with God". For God caused Christ, who himself knew nothing of sin, actually to *be* sin for our sakes, so that in Christ we might be made good with the goodness of God.
>
> As co-operators with God himself we beg you, then, not to fail to use the grace of God.
>
> (II Cor. 5: *16*–6: *1*)

But to get this message across was hard work, as it still is today, and St. Paul found himself fighting a tough spiritual battle in order to get people to accept the real liberty of the Gospel. You see, it was not only their sins and the ignorance that he was up against, but this queer unwillingness of the human heart to accept the fact that Christ really is willing to live within a man's personality.

St. Paul's letter goes on:

> The truth is that, although of course we lead normal human lives, the battle we are fighting is on the spiritual level. The very weapons we use are not those of human warfare but powerful in God's warfare for the destruction of the enemy's strongholds. Our battle is to bring down every deceptive fantasy and every imposing defence that men erect against the true knowledge of God. We even fight to capture every thought until it acknowledges the authority of Christ. (II Cor. 10: 3-5)

RECEIVING THE SPIRIT   The Purpose of God – 17

THE IDEA that the Christian life is not so much a strenuous performance but a living in harmony with the inward direction and reinforcement of the Spirit of God was, of course, no invention of St. Paul, though he was its untiring champion. Christ himself spoke of the readiness of God to give his own Spirit to those who were willing to receive him:

"The one who asks will always receive; the one who is searching will always find, and the door is opened to the man who knocks. Some of you are fathers, and if your son asks you for some fish, would you give him a snake instead; or if he asks you for an egg, would you make him a present of a scorpion? So, if you, for all your evil, know how to give good things to your children, how much more likely is it that your Heavenly Father will give the Holy Spirit to those who ask him!"

(Luke 11: *10–13*)

How beautifully simple and direct Jesus makes it! For those who are willing to receive the Spirit of God within their own personalities, it is not a matter of strenuous action, but of simple honest asking.

But of course the contact with him must be maintained, and in another passage, Jesus tells his followers how necessary it is to keep in close contact with him if they are to maintain the quality of their lives:

"When a man loves me, he follows my teaching. Then my Father will love him, and we will come to that man and make our home within him.

"I am the real vine, my Father is the vine-dresser. He removes any of my branches which are not bearing fruit and he prunes every branch that does bear fruit to increase its yield. Now, you have already been pruned by my words. You must go on growing in me and I will grow in you. For just as the branch cannot bear any fruit unless it shares the life of the vine, so you can produce nothing unless you go on growing in me. I am the vine itself, you are the branches. It is the man who shares my life and whose life I share who proves fruitful. For the plain fact is that apart from me you can do nothing at all. The man who does not share my life is like a branch that is broken off and withers away. He becomes just like the dry sticks that men pick up and use for firewood. But if you live your life in me, and my words live in your hearts, you can ask for whatever you like and it will come true for you. This is how my Father will be glorified – in your becoming fruitful and being my disciples.

"I have loved you just as the Father has loved me. You must go on living in my love. If you keep my commandments you will live in my love just as I have kept my Father's commandments and live in his love. I have told you this so that you can share my joy, and that your happiness may be complete."
(John 14: *23*, 15: *1-11*)

CHILDREN OF GOD The Purpose of God – 18

I HAVE said several things about what it means to a human being to have the very Spirit of God within him. Here is how St. Paul describes it, in a magnificent passage which needs no comment:

> All who follow the leading of God's Spirit are God's own sons. Nor are you meant to relapse into the old slavish attitude of fear – you have been adopted into the very family circle of God and you can say with a full heart, "Father, my Father". The Spirit himself endorses our inward conviction that

we really are the children of God. Think what that means. If we are his children we share his treasures, and all that Christ claims as his will belong to all of us as well! Yes, if we share in his sufferings we shall certainly share in his glory.

In my opinion whatever we may have to go through now is less than nothing compared with the magnificent future God has planned for us. The whole creation is on tiptoe to see the wonderful sight of the sons of God coming into their own. The world of creation cannot as yet see reality, not because it chooses to be blind, but because in God's purpose it has been so limited – yet it has been given hope. And the hope is that in the end the whole of created life will be rescued from the tyranny of change and decay, and have its share in that magnificent liberty which can only belong to the children of God!

It is plain to anyone with eyes to see that at the present time all created life groans in a sort of universal travail. And it is plain, too, that we who have a foretaste of the Spirit are in a state of painful tension, while we wait for that redemption of our bodies which will mean that at last we have realised our full sonship in him. We were saved by this hope, but in our moments of impatience let us remember that hope always means waiting for something that we do not yet possess. But if we hope for something we cannot see, then we must settle down to wait for it in patience.

The Spirit of God not only maintains this hope within us, but helps us in our present limitations. For example, we do not know how to pray worthily as sons of God, but his Spirit within us is actually praying for us in those agonising longings which can never find words. And God who knows the heart's secrets understands, of course, the Spirit's intention as he prays for those who love God.

Moreover we know that to those who love God, who are called according to his plan, everything that happens fits into a pattern for good.

In face of all this, what is there left to say? If God is for us, who can be against us? He who did not grudge his own Son but gave him up for us all – can we not trust such a God to give us, with him, everything else that we can need?

Who can separate us from the love of Christ? Can trouble, pain or persecution? Can lack of clothes and food, danger to life and limb, the threat of force of arms?

No, in all these things we win an overwhelming victory through him who has proved his love for us.

(Romans 8: *14-37*)

REAL LIFE IN GOD   The Purpose of God – 19

WHEN A man has the Spirit of God within him, his life is much more satisfying and "all-of-a-piece". The whole of his personality is moving in the same direction, not of course that he is already perfect, but that the Spirit of God gives him an unshakeable conviction that he knows where he's going. He certainly doesn't know all the answers, but being now consciously linked up with the timeless life of God, he is much better able to cope with the pressures and tensions of this little life. And he is much less likely to be taken in by the deceitful glamours of this passing world; he sees this life for what it is, a limited but necessary part of his existence as a son of God. But he never rests his weight upon this life, he never gives it his confidence, for he knows that his real life is in God. Let me quote from St. Paul again:

> For it is Christ Jesus as Lord whom we preach, not ourselves; we are your servants for Jesus' sake. God who first ordered light to shine in darkness has flooded our hearts with his light. We now can enlighten men only because we can give them knowledge of the glory of God, as we see it in the face of Jesus Christ.
> This priceless treasure we hold, so to speak, in a common earthenware jar – to show that the splendid power of it belongs to God and not to us. We are handicapped on all sides, but we are never frustrated; we are puzzled, but never in despair. We are persecuted, but we never have to stand it alone: we may be knocked down but we are never knocked out! Every day we experience something of the death of Jesus, so that we may also know the power of the life of Jesus in these bodies of ours ... The outward man does indeed suffer wear and tear, but every day the inward man receives fresh strength. These little troubles (which are really so transitory) are winning for us a permanent, glorious and solid reward out of all proportion to our pain. For we are looking all the time not at the visible things but at the invisible. The visible things are transitory: it is the invisible things that are really permanent.

We know, for instance, that if our earthly dwelling were taken down, like a tent, we have a permanent house in Heaven, made, not by man, but by God. In this present frame we sigh with deep longing for the heavenly house, for we do not want to face utter nakedness when death destroys our present dwelling – these bodies of ours. So long as we are clothed in this temporary dwelling we have a painful longing, not because we want just to get rid of these "clothes" but because we want to know the full cover of the permanent house that will be ours. We want our transitory life to be absorbed into the life that is eternal.

Now the power that has planned this experience for us is God, and he has given us his Spirit as a guarantee of its truth. This makes us confident, whatever happens. (II Cor. 4: 5–5: 6)

THE GREAT PLAN   The Purpose of God – 20

AS WE read the New Testament, something of the immense plan of God for mankind becomes apparent. God has not only shown himself in human form in Christ, but he gives freely his living Spirit to enable men to live as sons of God. We may look upon it as a huge patient scheme of reconciliation. On the one hand is man, living in ignorance and selfishness; and on the other hand is the steady unremitting pressure of the love of God, bringing men to see what they might be, and giving them the power to become sons of God in spite of every opposition within and without. These verses from St. Paul's letter to the Ephesians show how he caught glimpes of this vast and exciting purpose of God:

> Even though we were dead in our sins, God who is rich in mercy because of the great love he had for us, gave us life together with Christ – it is, remember, by grace and not by achievement that you are saved – and has lifted us right out of the old life to take our place with him in Christ Jesus in the Heavens. Thus he shows for all time the tremendous generosity of the grace and kindness he has expressed towards us in Christ Jesus. It was nothing you could or did achieve – it was God's gift of grace which saved you. No one can pride himself upon earning the love of God. The fact is that what we are we owe to the hand of God upon us. We are his workmanship, created in Christ Jesus to do those good deeds which God planned for us to do.
> So you are no longer outsiders or aliens, but fellow-citizens with every other Christian – you belong now to the household of God. Firmly beneath you is the foundation, God's messengers and prophets, the actual foundation-stone being Jesus Christ himself. In him each separate piece of building, properly fitting into its neighbour, grows together into a temple consecrated to God. You are all part of this building in which God himself lives by his Spirit.
> When I think of the greatness of this great plan, I fall on my knees before the Father (from whom all fatherhood, earthly or heavenly, derives its name), and I pray that out of the glorious richness of his resources he will enable you to know the strength of the Spirit's inner reinforcement – that

Christ may actually live in your hearts by your faith. And I pray that you, firmly fixed in love yourselves, may be able to grasp (with all Christians) how wide and deep and long and high is the love of Christ – and to know for yourselves that love so far beyond our comprehension. May you be filled through all your being with God himself!

(Ephes 2: *1*–3: *19*)

II

FAITH

Competition in Goodness

IT'S A strange thing, but a lot of people seem to imagine that life is a kind of competition in being good! They think that Christians and the people who go to church are saying to those who live without faith, without ever going to church – "Look at us, we're ever so much better than you!" Consequently, the non-Christian, the non-Church-goer, quite often says, – "I'm quite as good as So-and-so who calls himself a Christian and goes to church regularly". And then he thinks he's given a final and crushing reply to the whole Christian faith!

I really don't know where this idea of a "competition in being good" came from; it certainly isn't the Christian religion. After all, judging by ordinary standards, I can think straight away of a dozen good decent people who would never claim to hold the Christian faith and certainly never go to church, and they're very nice people. At the same time I can think of an equal number of people who *do* hold the Christian faith and who *do* go to church. They're full of faults and failings, of which they're well aware and which they're trying to overcome with the help of God. And they're very nice people too!

This "competition in goodness" idea is really quite beside the point. The fact is that a lot of decent-living people never seem to have any need of God. While among any group of Christians you'd be bound to find people who have sought God because they needed him, either because their own temperaments were too much for them, or because life faced them with overwhelming tragedy or difficulty, or simply because they found that, until they knew God, life was a pretty empty affair with no aim or purpose. The question of being "better" or "superior" to people outside the churches doesn't, in my experience arise at all.

Our Faith – a Visited Planet

The trouble is that many people seem to think that Christianity is based on the idea that "if you're a good boy you'll go to Heaven when you die". But when you come to examine it you find it's nothing of the kind. It's a much deeper affair, something much more important and much more far-reaching than that. For it means *believing*, and this is where all Christianity starts, *that we're living on a planet which has been personally visited by God himself, in human form, in the man Jesus*. Christians seriously believe that the vast power and wisdom behind this enormously complex Universe actually became a human being. So that you and I are living on a visited planet, a part of the Universe where God, as a matter of sober history, lived and died as a human being. And that's a staggering thing to believe.

Difficulties in believing

Now the modern astronomer, who is beginning to get some idea of the immeasurable vastness of the Universe around us, may find the Christian faith very hard to accept. For our little planet is so minute, so infinitesimal, compared with the boundless universe which surrounds us, that it seems almost laughable that the creator of the whole scheme could reduce himself to the stature of a man! I think there are two considerations which may make the Christian faith somewhat easier to accept.

First, although our little minds are filled with awe at displays of size and energy, we have no reason to suppose that size and energy are important in themselves, that is, in the eyes of the creator. As we learn a little bit from astronomy we may think we are in a rather frightening situation. But frightening to whom? Only, surely, to human beings. We cannot imagine that the infinite Spirit behind all life is in any way impressed by what frightens us! Moreover, even in human circumstances, size and energy can matter very little compared with the importance of people. If I go to Southampton to meet a special friend who has arrived from America on the *Queen*

Elizabeth, does it matter to me that that great ship has a million times more physical strength than my friend, or weighs ten million times as much? Not in the least! In fact, in the pleasure of meeting again we probably both forget all about the size and energy of the *Queen Elizabeth*.

In the second place, although I myself, like a great many other Christians, after a good deal of questing and thought, have come down solidly on the side of believing that God has been here, that Jesus Christ was who he claimed to be, yet I haven't the faintest idea what God has done, or plans to do, in other parts of his amazing Universe. As far as *this* world is concerned I am convinced that God expressed himself in Jesus Christ – that Jesus Christ is the right word *for human beings*. But if and how and when God expressed himself to other worlds, past, present or future, is none of my business. In fact, talking of other worlds, I sometimes think that when we start guessing about that kind of thing, we're getting a bit too big for our boots! And incidentally, wouldn't it be better to spend money on conquering such things as polio and cancer than on planning to visit the moon or Mars?

New Light on God

Now, once you honestly reach this conclusion that Christ was God – God revealed as fully as is possible, in a human being – you certainly don't know all the answers, but you have a remarkable amount of light to live by. For one thing, it revolutionises your conception of the character of God. You don't see him any longer as a remote and terrifying being insulated from human life. You see him as God who *so loved Man* that *he became Man*. It was not a put-up job. He did it properly, without supernatural advantages, and he lived and died in the sweat and pain of human life, This is not one of those pagan legends about one of the gods disguised as a human being: *this is the real thing*. And once you see what God really was and did and suffered, you begin to see what kind of a person he is, and you have a powerful clue to his long and patient purpose.

New Light on Man

But to be a Christian, that is, to hold this basic belief about God's visit, also changes your whole attitude towards Man. For Jesus Christ, who called himself the Son of God without hesitation, was also unashamedly the Son of Man. Again and again he shows in his teaching that love of God must never be separated from love of Man, fatally easy though that division is. Indeed, in his parable of the Last Judgement, we find him, who was both Son of God and Son of Man, insisting that the way men had treated people, even the least important people, was the way they had treated him. And because this is such a surprising judgement, the people in the parable are both amazed and horrified.

But such a standard of judgement on human behaviour is really only commonsense. For if God becomes Man, then the value of Man, to put it bluntly, immediately goes up enormously! People matter, even unlikeable and evil people, matter, since God has linked himself indissolubly with the human race. For by this Act of God men are lifted from being mere specimens of *homo sapiens* and may become sons of God with a future beyond our wildest imaginings. If you look upon your neighbour, or your enemy for that matter, as at least potentially the "son of God" it makes a fundamental change in your whole attitude towards him. In fact, the heart and essence of the Christian faith is to believe *differently*, differently about God and differently about Man. And once you accept the Christian faith, you find yourself becoming sure of all kinds of things that were previously only guess-work. I only have time to mention one, and that is the question of what is right and what is wrong, the question of standards and values.

New Values

I once heard a highly intelligent lady on the Brains' Trust, if I may quote from memory, say – "I try to be a good human being". Now such a remark is quite meaningless unless we know what a good human being is supposed to be. I imagine that the ideal of "a good human being" in a Communist country, which denies God and where individual human life is held quite cheap, is an entirely different conception from what is held in a Christian country. For, let us be quite honest about it, unless we know something about God, ideas of what is "good" and what is "human" are purely a matter of opinion, tradition, climate or even expediency! The lady on the Brains' Trust had, I am sure, a perfectly clear idea of what she meant by "a good human being", even though she disclaimed any religious faith. Nevertheless, *she is in fact the product of several centuries of Christian tradition.* And that goes for most of us too. Take away the Christian faith and no one knows for sure what is really "good". Who is to say that the Communist may not be right and we ourselves quite wrong in our ideas of goodness and humanity?

New Purpose

But although the recorded life of Christ gives the Christian reliable – and, to be honest, sometimes surprising – standards and values by which to live, he has a great deal more than that to help him in this difficult business of living. For once he commits himself to the way of life which Christ taught, he finds that Christ is no dead figure of history but a person, alive and contemporary. The Christian is no longer a tiny creature, living on an insignificant sphere in a vast and frightening Universe. He is no longer a man who sees no plan or purpose in life, who has no hope beyond the grave. For he finds himself linked to someone infinitely greater and wiser than himself. He sees the beginnings of a plan in which he is asked to co-operate, so vast that it almost takes his breath away. It is like being given a new dimension, for the Christian the horizon is suddenly lifted, and this little life is seen for what it is, only the temporary preparatory stage to the sharing of the timeless life of God. In the here-and-now he must certainly do all the good he can; certainly he is called to a life of self-giving love, of compassion and service. But he is forever delivered from being such a fool as to suppose that this life is everything, and that all his hopes and dreams are finished when his body dies.

Faith means Commitment

To become a Christian means, to start with, an act of faith. But as the months and the years pass and experience of God grows, what began as an honest, but rather tremulous, step becomes an unshakeable conviction. I have seen this happen so many times to so many people that I honestly don't know what the atheist and the agnostic mean when they say there is no "proof" of the existence of God. What sort of proof do they want? You can't write off the conviction and the experience of millions of people as mere imagination or as auto-suggestion.

But I think I know where the real trouble often lies. The uncomfortable fact is that *there is no proof without commitment*. You may think it unfair, but the plain fact is that you *cannot* know God for certain and you *cannot* experience the companionship of Christ unless and until you commit yourself to that way of living which Christ came to teach and to demonstrate. God, of course, will never assault your personality and you can, if you like, remain a cosy uncommitted agnostic all your days. But if you want to know God, if you want to co-operate with his purpose and to know beyond doubt your own high destiny as a son or daughter of God, Christ is the way in.

SIMPLE FAITH   Faith – 1

WHEN JESUS had finished these talks to the people, he came to Capernaum, where it happened that there was a man very seriously ill and in fact on the point of death. He was the slave of a centurion who thought very highly of him. When the centurion heard about Jesus, he sent some Jewish elders to him with the request that he would come and save his servant's life. When they came to Jesus, they urged him strongly to grant this request, saying that the centurion deserved to have this done for him. "He loves our nation and has built us a synagogue out of his own pocket", they said.

So Jesus went with them, but as he approached the house, the centurion sent some of his personal friends with the message,

"Don't trouble yourself, sir! I'm not important enough for you to come into my house – I didn't think I was fit to come to you in person. Just give the order, please, and my servant will recover. I am used to working under orders, and I have soldiers under me. I can say to one, 'Go', and he goes, or I can say to another, 'Come here', and he comes; or I can say to my slave, 'Do this job', and he does it".

These words amazed Jesus and he turned to the crowd who were following behind him, and said,

"I have never found faith like this anywhere, even in Israel!" (Mark 7: *1-9*)

Jesus was plainly both surprised and delighted by the faith of this Roman centurion. The soldier took it quite as a matter of course that, just as he knew how to give orders and expected them to be obeyed in military matters, so Jesus was the authority over the unseen forces which caused disease. To the soldier it was as simple as that.

I cannot help feeling that we have largely lost this simple direct faith in the power of Christ, and yet it appears again and again in the pages both of the Gospels and the Epistles. Of course you may think it was easy for people who saw and heard Christ in person to have faith in him, and yet the records show that a lot of them did not. However, apart from the Gospel records, there is plenty of evidence in the Epistles (which reflect the life of the early Church) to show how this faith in God transformed people, kept them going in spite of all kinds of troubles and difficulties, and gave their lives a real point and direction.

It really wouldn't be an exaggeration to say that this faith, this direct reaching out to touch the reality of God, and to depend upon it, is an absolute essential for the Christian life. "Without faith it is impossible to please him", said the author of the Epistle to the Hebrews. I don't think that is meant to be a threat so much as a plain statement of fact. We don't really begin to live our lives with God until we exercise this faculty which God has implanted in all of us, which the New Testament calls "faith". Have we got the courage to break through our habitual ways of thinking and believe like the centurion, simply and directly, in the power of God?

HEROES OF FAITH — Faith – 2

IT WAS because of his faith that Abel made a better sacrifice to God than Cain, and he had evidence that God looked upon him as a righteous man, whose gifts he could accept. And though Cain killed him, yet by his faith he still speaks to us today.

It was because of his faith that Enoch was promoted to the eternal world without experiencing death. He disappeared from this world because God promoted him, and before that happened his reputation was that "he pleased God". And without faith it is impossible to please him. The man who approaches God must have faith in two things, first that God exists and secondly that it is worth a man's while to try to find God.

It was through his faith that Noah, on receiving God's warning of impending disaster, reverently constructed an ark to save his household. This action of faith condemned the unbelief of the rest of the world, and won for Noah the righteousness before God which follows such a faith.

It was by faith that Abraham obeyed the summons to go out to a place which he would eventually possess, and he set out in complete ignorance of his destination. It was faith that kept him journeying like a foreigner through the land of promise, with no more home than the tents which he shared with Isaac and Jacob, co-heirs with him of the promise. For Abraham's eyes were looking forward to that city with solid foundations of which God himself is both architect and builder.

It was by faith that even Sarah gained the physical vitality to become a mother despite her great age, and she gave birth to a child when far beyond the normal years of child-bearing. She could do this because she believed that the one who had given the promise was utterly trustworthy. So it happened that from one man, who as a potential father was already considered dead, there arose a race "as numerous as the stars", as "countless as the sands of the sea-shore".

All these whom we have mentioned maintained their faith but died without actually receiving God's promises, though they had seen them in the distance, had hailed them as true and were quite convinced of their reality. They freely admitted that they lived on this earth as exiles and foreigners. Men who say that mean, of course, that their eyes are fixed upon their true home-land. The fact is that they longed for a better country altogether, nothing less than a heavenly one. And because of this faith of theirs, God is not ashamed to be called their God for in sober truth he has prepared for them a city. (Hebrews 11: *4–16*)

To some of us these heroes and heroines of more than two thousands years ago may seem very distant and unreal. The real point about them is that they exercised their faculty of faith even when prudence and commonsense would have held them back, and and held on to what they believed was the voice or direction of God. Prudence and commonsense are not bad things, but if we rely on them entirely we shall not be able to use that God-given faculty which the Bible calls "faith".

FAITH IS TESTED Faith – 3

THANK GOD, the God and Father of our Lord Jesus Christ, that in his great mercy we men have been born again into a life full of hope, through Christ's rising again from the dead! You can now hope for a perfect inheritance beyond the reach of change and decay, "reserved" in Heaven for you. And in the meantime you are guarded by the power of God operating through your faith, till you enter fully into the salvation which is all ready for the dénouement of the last day. This means tremendous joy to you, I know, even though at present you are temporarily harrassed by all kinds of trials and temptations. This is no accident – it happens to prove your faith, which is infinitely more valuable than gold, and gold, as you know, even though it is ultimately perishable, must be purified by fire. This proving of your faith is planned to result in praise and honour and glory in the day when Jesus Christ reveals himself. And though you have never seen him, yet I know that you love him. At present you trust him without being able to see him, and even now he brings you a joy that words cannot express and which has in it a hint of the glories of Heaven; and all the time you are receiving the result of your faith in him – the salvation of your own souls. The prophets of old did their utmost to discover and obtain this salvation. They did not find it, but they prophesied of this grace that has now come to you. . . . It is these very matters which have been made plain to you by those who preached the gospel to you by the Holy Spirit sent from Heaven – and these are facts to command the interest of the very angels!

So brace up your minds, and, as men who know what they are doing, rest the full weight of your hopes on the grace that will be yours when Jesus Christ reveals himself.   (I Peter 1: *3–13*)

For some reason that we do not understand, our faith in God, as Peter here warns his readers, is liable to be tested by what he calls "all kinds of trials and temptations". Christian experience was the same then as it is now. There are always people who are ready to laugh at our believing in the power of someone whom we cannot see, and there is part of our own nature which is inclined to agree with them. Faith has to be developed by actual experience. We have to believe where we cannot see, and we have to trust in spite of what we may be feeling. This helps us to put on spiritual "muscle", as it were, so that as the years go by our solid confidence in God becomes more and more strong and dependable. We learn that we can rest our full weight upon the completely dependable God.

FAITH GROWS BY TESTING Faith – 4

WHEN ALL kinds of trials and temptations crowd into your lives, my brothers, don't resent them as intruders, but welcome them as friends! Realise that they come to test your faith and to produce in you the quality of endurance. But let the process go on until that endurance is fully developed, and you will find you have become men of mature character with the right sort of independence. And if, in the process, any of you does not know how to meet any particular problem he has only to ask God – who gives generously to all men without making them feel foolish or guilty – and he may be quite sure that the necessary wisdom will be given him. But he must ask in sincere faith without secret doubts as to whether he really wants God's help or not. The man who trusts God, but with inward reservations, is like a wave of the sea, carried forward by the wind one moment and driven back the next. That sort of man cannot hope to receive anything from the Lord, and the life of a man of divided loyalty will reveal instability at every turn.

. . . The man who patiently endures the temptations and trials that come to him is the truly happy man. For once his testing is complete he will receive the crown of life which the Lord has promised to all who love him.

A man must not say when he is tempted, "God is tempting me". For God cannot be tempted by evil, and does not himself tempt anyone. No, a man's temptation is due to the pull of his own inward desires, which can be enormously attractive. His own desire takes hold of him, and that produces sin. And sin in the long run means death – make no mistake about that, brothers of mine! But every good endowment that we possess and every complete gift that we have received must come from above, from the Father of all lights, with whom there is never the slightest variation or shadow of inconsistency. (James 1: *2–17*)

Here we find James speaking in just the same way as Peter did about the testing of a Christian's faith. We are not to regard this process with alarm or resentment, but as something which in the long run will prove to be our friend. Of course it often does not look like that. Our faith is bent this way and that, it is pulled, it is hammered – whatever picture you like to use. But in the long run, the man with a single-minded trust in God finds he has developed a quality of spiritual endurance.

Part of the testing will come, not from the ordinary circumstances of life, but from the lower desires of our own natures. We must be careful, says James, not to attribute these temptations to God, though it is perfectly true that he allows them to happen. Whether it is the testing of circumstance or the temptations of our own natures or temperaments, the Christian has to learn to maintain his steadfast trust in God. That is how his faith grows.

THE BATTLE OF FAITH   Faith – 5

IN CONCLUSION, be strong – not in yourselves but in the Lord, in the power of his boundless resource. Put on God's complete armour so that you can successfully resist all the devil's methods of attack. For our fight is not against any physical enemy: it is against organisations and powers that are spiritual. We are up against the unseen power that controls this dark world, and spiritual agents from the very headquarters of evil. Therefore you must wear the whole armour of God that you may be able to resist evil in its day of power, and that even when you have fought to a standstill you may still stand your

ground. Take your stand then with truth as your belt, righteousness your breastplate, the gospel of peace firmly on your feet, salvation as your helmet and in your hand the sword of the Spirit, the Word of God. Above all be sure you take faith as your shield, for it can quench every burning missile the enemy hurls at you. Pray at all times with every kind of spiritual prayer, keeping alert and persistent as you pray for all Christ's men and women.
(Ephes 6: *10–18*)

In this well-known passage, Paul is emphasising the battle that every Christian has to wage. There are forces unseen, but very much to be reckoned with, which would fill us with doubt and mistrust, take away our faith, and smother us with fear and anxiety. Our job as Christians is to resist the smothering power of evil forces by keeping ourselves fit and alert spiritually by tapping the resources of God.

This battle of faith is a life-long battle, and of course sometimes it is much harder than others. There are times when it is easy for us to believe in God, in his purpose for us, and in his ultimate triumph. But there are other times when skies are overcast, when spiritual things seem to have lost their meaning and God himself appears to be far away. This is where we are to do battle, to go on actively, and even aggressively, believing in the goodness and loving purpose of God; never mind what happens or what we feel.

Sometimes again we make great progress, at other

times we seem to do no more than maintain our footing. But the practised Christian soldier can at least do this. Paul says, "Even when you have fought to a standstill you may still stand your ground".

This battle of faith is one to which all Christians are committed. We are all in it together. And behind us all and within us all is the boundless resource of God. So keep fighting the good fight of faith!

THE BATTLE IS WORTHWHILE   Faith –6

God is always against the proud, but he is always ready to give grace to the humble. So, humble yourselves under God's strong hand, and in his own good time he will lift you up. You can throw the whole weight of your anxieties upon him, for you are his personal concern.

Be self-controlled and vigilant always, for your enemy the devil is always about, prowling like a lion roaring for its prey. Resist him, standing firm in your faith and remember that the strain is the same for all your fellow-Christians in other parts of the world. And after you have borne these sufferings a very little while, the God of all grace, who has called you to share his eternal splendour through Christ, will himself make you whole and secure and strong.   (I Peter 5: *5b–11*)

Now a passage from Paul's first letter to Timothy:

But you, the man of God, keep clear of such things. Set your heart not on riches, but on goodness, Christ-likeness, faith, love, patience and humility. Fight the worth-while battle of the faith, keep your grip on that life eternal to which you have been called, and to which you boldly professed your loyalty before many witnesses. I charge you in the sight of God who gives life to all things, and Christ Jesus who fearlessly witnessed to the truth before Pontius Pilate, to keep your commission clean and above reproach until the final coming of Christ. (I Timothy 6: *11–14*)

It is interesting to see how the experience of Christians in differing circumstances is basically the same. As Peter wrote, "The strain is the same for all your fellow-Christians in other parts of the world". And in a way it is not only interesting but exciting, because these words of Peter and Paul are good sound advice today, nearly two thousand years afterwards. It is truly thrilling to know that these words apply to us because we are fighting the same "worthwhile battle of faith", as Paul calls it, as those early Christians fought long ago. I believe it is a really worthwhile battle of faith, though the world, the flesh and the devil will always try to make us believe that it is not worthwhile. But what are we really doing as we fight this fight, as we draw on the resources of God and use the weapons that he has given us? In the first place we are deepening and strengthening our own hold upon God, and that is a thing which is not only useful to ourselves, but may be a tremendous help to somebody else who hardly knows God at all. In the second place, as a kind of by-product, and maybe without our knowing it, we shall be witnessing to a largely unbelieving world that there is such a person as God, and that the Christian religion is a workable and worthwhile way of living.

SAVED BY FAITH Faith – 7

IN THE course of his letter to the Romans Paul says:

> Now this counting of faith for righteousness was not recorded simply for Abraham's credit, but as a divine principle which should apply to us as well. Faith is to be reckoned as righteousness to us also, who believe in him who raised from the dead Jesus, our Lord, who was delivered to death for our sins and raised again to secure our justification. Since then it is by faith that we are justified, let us grasp the fact that we *have* peace with God through our Lord Jesus Christ. Through him we have confidently entered into this new relationship of grace, and here we take our stand, in happy certainty of the glorious things he has for us in the future.
> This doesn't mean, of course, that we have only a hope of future joys – we can be full of joy here and now even in our trials and troubles. Taken in the right spirit these very things will give us patient endurance; this in turn will develop a mature character, and a character of this sort produces a steady hope, a hope that will never disappoint us. Already

we have some experience of the love of God flooding through our hearts by the Holy Spirit given to us. And we can see that it was while we were powerless to help ourselves that Christ died for sinful men. In human experience it is a rare thing for one man to give his life for another, even if the latter be a good man, though there have been a few who have had the courage to do it. Yet the proof of God's amazing love is this: that it was *while we were sinners* that Christ died for us. (Romans 4: *23*–5: *8*)

This quality of faith, this reaching out and holding on to the reality of God is, Paul explains to us, more valuable in the sight of God than any of our good deeds. Indeed, he tells us a great many times in this letter to the Romans and in many other places that we cannot ever *earn* our acceptance with God. We can only believe that God himself has provided the means of our reconciliation with himself through Christ.

This is another aspect of the battle of faith. Our own minds continually suggest that we ought to justify ourselves before God by our good actions, even though we know from experience that this is a hopeless task. Paul's particular teaching – and I believe him to have been inspired in giving us this teaching – is that we cannot possibly save ourselves. Christ himself has made the bridge between God and Man which we could never build. Christianity is a matter of believing rather than achieving. We must drop all our confidence in our own efforts and put our entire trust in Christ; that is how we are "saved by faith".

AT PEACE WITH GOD   Faith – 8

IN HIS letter to the Ephesians Paul writes:

To you, who were spiritually dead all the time that you drifted along on the stream of this world's ideas of living, and obeyed its unseen ruler, (who is still operating in those who do not respond to the truth of God), to you Christ has given life! We all lived like that in the past, and followed the impulses and imaginations of our evil nature, being in fact under the wrath of God by nature, like everyone else. But even though we were dead in our sins God, who is rich in mercy, because of the great love he had for us, gave us life together with Christ – it is, remember, by grace and not by achievement that you are saved – and has lifted us right out of the old life to take our place with him in Christ Jesus in the Heavens. Thus he shows for all time the tremendous generosity of the grace and kindness he has expressed towards us in Christ Jesus. It was nothing you could or did achieve – it was God's gift of grace which saved you. No one can pride himself upon earning the love of God. The fact is that what we are we owe to the hand of God upon us. For we are his workmanship created in Christ Jesus to do those good deeds which God planned for us to do. . . . You were without Christ, you were utter strangers to God's chosen community, Israel, and you had no knowledge of, or right to, the promised agreements. You had nothing to look forward to and no God to whom you could turn. But now, through the blood of Christ, you who were once outside the pale are with us inside the circle of God's love in Christ Jesus. For Christ is our living peace. He has made a unity of the conflicting elements of Jew and gentile by breaking down the barrier which lay between us. By his sacrifice he removed the hostility of the Law, with all its commandments and rules, and made in himself out of the two, Jew and gentile, one new man, thus producing peace. For he reconciled both to God by the sacrifice of one body on the cross, and by this act made utterly irrelevant the antagonism between them. Then he came and told both you who were far from God and us who were near that the war was over. And it is through him that both of us now can approach the Father in the one Spirit.

So you are no longer outsiders or aliens, but fellow-citizens with every other Christian – you belong now to the household of God.

(Ephes. 2: *1-19*)

Here Paul is making plain to his converts that whether they are Jews or Gentiles they are at peace with God, not through their own efforts, but through God's astonishing generosity in Christ. The same thing is completely true for us today, and it is a truth that we grasp and hold on to by faith. If we are to know peace with God we have got to drop not only our pretences but all our strivings and achievements and accept his boundless generosity.

TEMPORARY HOUSING — Faith – 9

ONE OF the things that we have to do as Christians in fighting our daily battle of faith is to remember that we are only living temporarily in these physical bodies. What we do in these bodies is of course important, but our actual physical bodies themselves are only a temporary housing for the everlasting spirit that God has given to each one of us. We do the best we can in what St. Paul calls "these temporary dwellings", but we look forward hopefully to the time when we shall be set free from the limitations of the present earthly body and our eternal spirits are clothed in bodies fit for eternity.

This is how St. Paul put it in his second letter to the Corinthians:

> The outward man does indeed suffer wear and tear, but every day the inward man receives fresh strength. These little troubles (which are really so transitory) are winning for us a permanent, solid and glorious reward out of all proportion to our pain. For we are looking all the time not at the visible things but at the invisible. The visible things are transitory: it is the invisible things that are really permanent.
> We know, for instance, that if our earthly dwellings were taken down, like a tent, we have a permanent house in Heaven, made, not by man, but by God. In this present frame we sigh with deep

longing for the heavenly house, for we do not want to face utter nakedness when death destroys our present dwelling – these bodies of ours. So long as we are clothed in this temporary dwelling we have a painful longing, not because we want just to get rid of these "clothes", but because we want to know the full cover of the permanent house that will be ours. We want our transitory life to be absorbed into the life that is eternal.

Now the power that has planned this experience for us is God, and he has given us his Spirit as a guarantee of its truth. This makes us confident, whatever happens. We realise that being "at home" in the body means that to some extent we are "away" from the Lord, for we have to live by trusting him without seeing him. We are so sure of this that we would really rather be "away" from the body and be "at home" with the Lord.

It is our aim, therefore, to please him, whether we are "at home" or "away". For every one of us will have to stand without pretence before Christ our judge, and we shall be rewarded for what we did when we lived in our bodies, whether it was good or bad.   (II Cor. 4: *16*–5: *10*)

MAINTAINING FAITH   Faith – 10

ONE FINAL word about this Christian quality of "faith" – that faculty of reaching out and holding on to things which are believed but not seen. Perhaps I have made it seem rather a tough struggle. That is because I know that, for some of us, it *is* hard work to maintain faith in God.

There are at least two things that we can do to help our faith during these difficult days. One is to think of people who have gone before us and have fought this same fight and won. The other is to remember that Christ himself is the author and finisher of our faith. He stimulated that faculty of faith which is implanted in us all, and he is the one who will maintain our faith whatever may come, and bring it to the end where faith is "swallowed up in sight".

Both these truths are brought home to us in this inspiring passage from the Epistle to the Hebrews:

> And what other examples shall I give? There is simply not time to continue by telling the stories of Gideon, Barak, Samson and Jephtha; of David, Samuel and the prophets. Through their faith these men conquered kingdoms, ruled in justice and proved the truth of God's promises. They shut the mouths of lions, they quenched the furious blaze of fire, they escaped from death itself. From being weaklings they became strong men and mighty warriors; they routed whole armies of foreigners. Women received their dead raised to life again, while others were tortured and refused to be ransomed, because they wanted to deserve a more honourable resurrection in the world to come. Others were exposed to the test of public mockery and flogging, and to the torture of being left bound in prison. They were killed by stoning, by being

sawn in two; they were tempted by specious promises of release and then were killed with the sword. Many became refugees with nothing but sheepskins or goatskins to cover them. They lost everything and yet were spurned and ill-treated by a world that was too evil to see their worth. They lived as vagrants in the desert, on the mountains, or in caves or holes in the ground.

All these won a glowing testimony to their faith, but they did not then and there receive the fulfilment of the promise. God had something better planned for our day, and it was not his plan that they should reach perfection without us.

Surrounded then as we are by these serried ranks of witnesses, let us strip off everything that hinders us, as well as the sin which dogs our feet, and let us run the race that we have to run with patience, our eyes fixed on Jesus the source and the goal of our faith. For he himself endured a cross and thought nothing of its shame because of the joy he knew would follow his suffering; and he is now seated at the right hand of God's throne. Think constantly of him enduring all that sinful men could say against him, and you will not lose your purpose or your courage. (Hebrews 11: *32*–12: *3*)

III
HOPE

Disillusion

IF WE are going to live at all happily it is essential that we have a real, solid, reasonable hope at the heart of our living. Yet everybody knows that hope is one of those things which is in rather short supply these days. Well within my own lifetime the atmosphere of people's thinking has changed enormously – at any rate, as far as my own country of England is concerned.

For example, I have in my house several bound volumes of popular magazines dated in the early 1900's, just before I was born. These magazines are beautifully produced and make fascinating reading, for their carefree optimism, reflecting the spirit of those times, went right on to the outbreak of the First World War in 1914. Britain was rich and powerful, with a far-flung Empire; most trades seemed to be booming; the cost of living by our standards was fantastically cheap and income tax fantastically low. In addition, science was beginning to be applied to domestic and industrial problems, so that in many of the articles in these magazines you can read prophesies of such things as broadcasting and television, and "flying-machines", as they called them then, and even of helicopters. In fact you get the general impression that the dark ages are now safely behind us and that, by the light of science, mankind is now going to stride forward into unimaginable happiness. Of course, one of the great writers and prophets of those days, a man who put all his faith in humanity enlightened by science, was Mr. H. G. Wells, who died not so very long ago.

This safe, comfortable world with all its boundless optimism was shattered for ever by the 1914–18 war. I don't think ever again has that hopeful, almost bumptiously hopeful, atmosphere re-appeared in this country. Quickly or slowly, people began to see that science by itself is not enough, that trust in human nature by itself is not enough. H. G. Wells himself died in bitter disillusionment having just completed a book written out of his frantic disappointment. He called it – *Mind at the End of its Tether*.

The Second World War put a final end to any easy hopes or shallow optimism, and except in places which are particularly fortunate or where people don't think or read about what is happening to the world, you won't find today any of those shining hopes of the early 1900's.

Hope – and Wishful Thinking

Now I am no prophet of gloom, but I think I must point out now the difference between hope and, what we used to call in the last world war, "wishful thinking". Hope is based on realities – and in the end on God, the great reality. But wishful thinking, though it often sounds like hope, is nothing more than what we should like to happen. Now all of us, myself included, say, "We hope so-and-so" – when all we really mean is that we *wish* so-and-so may happen. I don't think this matters very much myself so long as we are quite sure of the difference in our own minds between expressing a wish like that and having a hope with real grounds behind it. For example, a young man may say, "I hope I have got through this exam". If he has worked hard and done a good paper, the hope is perfectly genuine. But if in fact he has done little or no work beforehand and answered the paper carelessly, it is not a genuine hope. It is merely an expression of his wishes.

Now naturally, being human beings, we all do this kind of thing from time to time. A man may quite naturally say, "I hope I don't die of some painful disease", or "I hope I don't live to be a burden to my relations". This is perfectly understandable and right – but not a hope. It is only what he wishes may happen.

Genuine Hope

Sometimes we touch the border-line between wishful thinking and hope. For example, if we go and see a friend who is ill we probably say when we leave, "Well, I hope you will soon be better". This is a perfectly natural kindly sentiment, and we sincerely mean it. It does however remain a wish unless, as soon as we get a quiet moment, we turn our love and sympathy and good wishes into a prayer for that friend's recovery. The wish becomes a hope the moment it is linked to the love and purpose of God. In fact, if you think about it, almost all that goes by the name of hope is merely wishful expectation. It only becomes genuine hope when it rests upon God. That is why I don't think you will find a single instance of the word "hope" being used in the New Testament unless it is connected with faith in God.

Genuine Hopes – and Pious Wishes

There is a peculiarly nauseating form of so-called hope which you will sometimes find, even in the best circles. People will say, for example, "I hope they will soon find a cure for cancer", but they wouldn't dream of giving a penny to the work of a Cancer Research Fund. Or they will say – "I hope something is done for all those thousands and thousands of poor refugees and homeless people over there in Europe."

But not one in a hundred who expresses such a hope does anything about it to make it come true.

Do you remember how St. James in his Epistle – writing, you will recall, nearly two thousand years ago – severely criticises this pious kind of hope. He says, in effect, that if you should see people cold or hungry or without proper clothes, and you say, "Well, God bless you – I hope you'll soon be all right," what good in the world is that? St. James is very downright, and has no use for the kind of faith or hope which simply expresses a pious wish and does nothing whatever about it. I mean, to bring it down to a fine point, it is only too easy for us to say, "Oh, I do hope Mrs. So-and-So is going on all right." We are perfectly sincere, but how much better if we take a little time and trouble to go and see Mrs. So-and-So, and find out if there is something we can do for her. We ought to beware of pious wishes unless we are prepared to make them genuine hopes.

Hopes of Heaven

Now even when you come to people inside the Church, the people whom I have been trying to serve and help for over twenty years, you often come across wishful thinking instead of genuine hope. People will say, for instance, "I certainly hope I get to Heaven," and I haven't any doubt that they wish that they will. But when you talk to them you find that very often they have never taken the trouble to find out what the New Testament has to say about the terms on which a human being can share the timeless life of God, which is what Heaven is. Not only have they not bothered to study the New Testament for themselves, but they have built up in their minds an idea that, if you avoid certain conspicuous sins, and on the whole do rather more good than harm in the world, then somehow or other you will get to Heaven.

You will certainly not find any endorsement of this point of view in any part of the New Testament, and yet how common it is! Those who hold it need desperately to exchange a wishful thought for a solid and dependable hope. And that's easy enough to do. Read, for example, the inspired words of St. John's Gospel and you will see quite plainly what I mean.

Hoping for the Best

Now hopefulness and optimism are very useful qualities with which to tackle the difficulties and strains of life. Take illness, for example. I am quite sure that any doctor would prefer a hopeful patient to a despairing one; and, of course, other things being equal, the chances of recovery are very much greater to the hopeful than they are to the despairing one. I am not trying to belittle hopefulness in the least, and I have often been amazed at the cheerfulness and optimism displayed by people under the most appalling difficulties. But hoping for the best is a very much stronger and more solid thing altogether if it rests upon the good purpose of God.

Dark Tunnels

Most of us, sooner or later in life, have to go through what we might call dark tunnels, whether of pain, or adverse circumstances, or bereavement, or natural anxiety over someone we love. And when it comes we say to ourselves, "I do hope I shall come through this all right." But do we mean hope, real hope, or is that just a wish? Have we any reason, any good, solid dependable reason for hope? Can we, so to speak, see the light at the other end of the tunnel? Believe me, I do know what I'm talking about here and I can tell you that if your whole life is honestly committed, body and soul, to your creator, who is also your Father and your Saviour – in the best sense your true lover – you can have real hope. You need not be lonely any more, and you need not be afraid any more, for you have not got to rely on the tension of your own screwed-up courage. You can relax, instead, upon the God of hope.

Once, some years ago, I myself went through a very dark tunnel indeed. And the words which came into my mind were these – "When thou passest through the waters I will be with thee, and through the rivers they shall not overflow thee." I rested my full weight on that promise and God brought me through that tunnel. A great many times since then I have passed that promise on to people in hospital or at home and, as simply as I could, urged them to rest their whole weight upon the goodness and the love of God. That is where hope, real hope, springs from. And Paul is perfectly right in calling God "The God of hope".

Hope – and Faith

I expect it has become obvious by now that hope and faith are very closely linked together. Without God human hope is really no more than wishful thinking and is very frequently disappointed. I have already mentioned that brilliant writer and scientific humanist, H. G. Wells, a man who placed his faith and his hope in humanity enlightened by science. But he died in bitter disappointment. And, of course, he is not alone in that. Thousands of people have thought that all that human beings need is knowledge and skill, and then a new world will happen almost automatically. But they too have grown disappointed and disillusioned. Of course, this is not so obvious when you are very young. Indeed, a great many people start off in life, when they are young and energetic and full of ideals, with high hopes. But where there is no faith in God, where the hope is not linked to the purpose of God, I myself have met many middle-aged people, both men and women, thoroughly cynical and disillusioned about human nature, that is, human nature without God, and very possibly their own human nature has let them down!

By shutting your eyes to certain unpleasant sides of life, and, if you are lucky enough, possessing good health and plenty of money, you may preserve a certain brittle optimism all your life. But if you are really down-to-earth, really down in the sweat and dust of the arena, so to speak, the odds are very heavy that you will lose your hopes and many of your ideals by the time that you are middle-aged. That is, if you are living your life without God. For, after all, where are the springs of fresh life to come from, once the energy and romance of youth has departed? Who is going to supply the shining vision and the worthwhile goal? Most important of all, who is going to supply the energy, the power to keep alive the flame of hope in a despairing world? Frankly, I don't see the answer in any human institutions, or in any ideology. I can only see hope, real hope, coming from the living purposeful Spirit of God.

Indomitable Hope

It is very remarkable to me that the New Testament is so full of hope. In the Epistles, for instance, it shines and sparkles on almost every page. And yet the men who wrote these unforgettable letters were often in danger, acute personal danger, frequently in ill-health, and indeed the people to whom they were writing were quite often in danger, for the mere fact that they were Christians. Incidentally, these letters are one of the finest pieces of evidence for the faith that I think we possess.

I often want to ask non-Christians – how do you explain the exuberant hope of this New Testament Christianity? If, as you suggest, Christianity is a myth, or cannot be worked out in practice, how do you account for these plainly transformed lives, and above all for this indomitable hopefulness? For remember, no one disputes the genuineness of most of the New Testament Epistles.

Well, of course, people may retort that times were easier then, the world was younger, life was less complicated. Life was certainly less complicated, but I'm pretty certain it wasn't less difficult. The then known world was inconceivably corrupt by modern standards, human life was cheap, there were few whom you could trust, and to be a Christian at all was in itself frequently a danger. No, I know they had not got the menace of the hydrogen bomb before them. But if I had to choose between bodily annihilation by a hydrogen bomb and being driven naked into an arena to be torn to pieces by wild beasts, as many of them were, I am pretty certain I should choose the modern horror!

No, times in New Testament days were not in the least hopeful, but the Christians possessed in God an unquenchable hope. This, I think, rested on two main certainties which I should like us all to recapture today. And, of course, they are both based on the certainty of God as revealed through Jesus Christ.

Good News

The first of these bases for hope is the hope for the individual, forgiven, remade and empowered by the living Christ. Paul and his friends and contemporaries had seen this greatest of all miracles – the changing of human nature – happening so often that, though they never regarded it as commonplace, yet they did regard the power of God as dependable and demonstrable. All problems are, in the end, problems of human nature; and these men knew for themselves, and had observed for themselves, human nature being changed by something, or rather, by someone, invisible, certainly, but completely dependable.

Here is the challenge that faces us. Have we given up hope for ourselves? Have we lapsed into a dreary compromise, where every straight line is blurred and all colours dulled to an unhappy grey? Have we, after repeated attempts to reform, decided that there is nothing we can do about it?

To me, to you, as individuals, Jesus Christ is our hope. Too often we think of religion as merely a matter of being good or of keeping difficult rules. But Christianity is never that – it is Good News. It is not good news to be told that you are a sinner. You probably know that already. But it *is* Good News to be told that you can stand up and walk forward as a son or daughter of God because there is a living dependable power, the power of Christ, readily available for you. God has not changed through the centuries, you know; and many of those places like Corinth and Ephesus had sunk far lower than you or I are ever likely to have sunk. But the Good News came to them: and the Good News comes to us. God offers us through Christ the reconciliation we could never make, the forgiveness we could never earn – that sense of being at one with God which all our strivings can never produce. And, what is more, if we are prepared to open our hearts and minds to the living Spirit of Christ, he will transform us from within.

This is no conjuring trick, but it is a miracle. For the very thing which all the clever people in the world say – "You can't change human nature" – is proved to be false by the thousands and thousands of people who have proved the living power of Christ.

Our Hope in God

The second basis on which New Testament Christians set their hope was their certainty of sharing the timeless life of God. They had this feeling so strongly that it didn't really matter to the best of them what happened to their bodies or possessions, for they themselves were linked to God through Christ. Paul had this hope developed in him to such a pitch that to all intents and purposes it was a certainty. When he faces death he says it will only be "to depart and be with Christ, which is far better".

It seems to me that these early Christians had, so to speak, shifted their deposit account into Heaven, into the spiritual realm where God eternally exists. They lived on this earth as temporary residents only, perfectly prepared to enjoy the good, or endure the bad, but not taken in by either. Their real hope lay far beyond this temporary realm of time and space.

Their hope was set in God himself.

Can we not allow the God of hope to fill us with joy and peace in our faith, as the early Christians did? There is no change in God. The hope for the individual soul, and thereby the hope for human society, remains constant. The transforming power of Christ is the same as it always was; and in him we have that bed-rock hope, that anchor for the soul which enables us to face all life's ills and accidents without despair. What is the matter with us? God is still there, and God is still the only sure and certain ground for hope, either in this world or in the world to come.

GENUINE HOPE   Hope – 1

BEFORE WE can even begin to consider the Christian virtue of hope we must be quite clear in our minds what hope really is.

Let me remind you, then, that a lot that goes by

the name of hope is really wishful thinking. A man may hope to win a fortune, but unless he has reasonable grounds for such hoping, this is no more than a wishful thought. And people often say such things as, "I hope everything will turn out all right"; but unless they have some grounds for their confidence it really is no more than saying, "I *wish* that it may turn out all right."

But we find that the hope which shines in the pages of the New Testament is of the genuine variety – it is held by faith. Paul talks about the sustaining hope which God has inspired in his heart and can inspire in our hearts as well:

> In my opinion whatever we may have to go through now is less than nothing compared with the magnificent future God has planned for us. The whole creation is on tiptoe to see the wonderful sight of the sons of God coming into their own. The world of creation cannot as yet see reality, not because it chooses to be blind, but because in God's purpose it has been so limited – yet it has been given hope. And the hope is that in the end the whole of created life will be rescued from the tryanny of change and decay, and have its share in that magnificent liberty which can only belong to the children of God!
>
> It is plain to anyone with eyes to see that at the present time all created life groans in a sort of universal travail. And it is plain, too, that we who have a foretaste of the Spirit are in a state of painful tension, while we wait for that redemption of our bodies which will mean that at last we have realised

our full sonship in him. We were saved by this hope, but in our moments of impatience let us remember that hope always means waiting for something that we do not yet possess. But if we hope for something we cannot see, then we must settle down to wait for it in patience.

The Spirit of God not only maintains this hope within us, but helps us in our present limitations. For example, we do not know how to pray worthily as sons of God, but his Spirit within us is actually praying for us in those agonising longings which never find words. And God who knows the heart's secrets understands, of course, the Spirit's intention as he prays for those who love God.

Moreover we know that to those who love God, who are called according to his plan, everything that happens fits into a pattern for good.

(Romans 8: *18–28*)

RADIANT WITH HOPE   Hope – 2

WE WHO have strong faith ought to shoulder the burden of the doubts and qualms of others and not just to go our own sweet way. Our actions should mean the good of others – should help them to build up their characters. For even Christ did not choose his own pleasure, but as it is written:

The reproaches of them that reproached thee fell upon me.

For all those words which were written long ago are meant to teach us today; that when we read in the scriptures of the endurance of men and of all the help that God gave them in those days, we may be encouraged to go on hoping in our own time. May the God who inspires men to endure, and gives them a Father's care, give you a mind united towards one another because of your common loyalty to Jesus Christ. And then, as one man, you will sing from the heart the praises of God the Father of our Lord Jesus Christ. So, open your hearts to one another as Christ has opened his heart to you, and God will be glorified.

Christ was made a servant of the Jews to prove God's trustworthiness, since he personally implemented the promises made long ago to the fathers, and also that the gentiles might bring glory to God for his mercy to them. It is written:

Therefore will I give praise unto thee among the gentiles and sing unto thy name.

May the God of hope fill *you* with joy and peace in your faith, that, by the power of the Holy Spirit, your whole life and outlook may be radiant with hope. (Romans 15: *1–13*)

To keep up our hopes Paul's inspired words recommend us to look back at the scriptures and see how God has helped and encouraged those who have put their faith in him. But it is not only at the scriptures that it is wise to look back. We can often look back at our own lives, at the times over which we used to be so worried and anxious, and see how God led us faithfully onwards. In other words, a good sound reason for hope in the future is past experience of God's dependability, both other people's and our own.

But we have not only got to depend on reminding ourselves, for God himself, as Paul assures us here, is the "God of Hope". He fills us with true optimism since his plans for us are always the very best that can be. Notice that *he* fills us with hope. It is not a quality that we have to generate on our own, though we can certainly help to put ourselves in the right frame of mind by recollecting God's faithfulness in the past.

Listen again to Paul's words:

that, by the power of the Holy Spirit, your whole life and outlook may be radiant with hope.

What a warm and glowing thought to take with us into another day!

GOD'S RELIABILITY Hope – 3

WE FEEL sure that you, whom we love, are capable of better things and will enjoy the full experience of salvation. God is not unfair: he will not lose sight of all that you have done, nor of the loving labour which you have shown for his sake in looking after fellow-Christians (as you are still doing). It is our earnest wish that every one of you should show a similar keenness in fully grasping the hope that is within you, until the end. We do not want any of you to grow slack, but to follow the example of those who through sheer patient faith came to possess the promises.

When God made his promise to Abraham he swore by himself, for there was no one greater by whom he could swear, and he said:

Surely blessing I will bless thee

And multiplying I will multiply thee.

And then Abraham, after patient endurance, found the promise true.

Among men it is customary to swear by something greater than ourselves. And if a statement is confirmed by an oath, that is the end of all quibbling. So in this matter, God, wishing to show beyond doubt that his plan was unchangeable, confirmed it with an oath. So that by two utterly immutable things, the word of God and the oath of God, who cannot lie, we who are refugees from this dying world might have a source of strength, and might grasp the hope that he holds out to us. This hope we hold as the utterly reliable anchor for our souls, fixed in the innermost shrine of Heaven, where Jesus has already entered on our behalf.

(Hebrews 6: *9–20*)

This passage has a very Jewish flavour, which is not surprising, considering that it was written in the first place to Jewish Christians! The author is really saying two things. First, that men must not grow slack but grasp the hope that God has given them firmly, patiently and steadfastly. People like Abraham in the Old Testament, for example, were given a hope and had to hold on to that hope by sheer patient faith. And there are times in life when we have to do exactly the same.

The second point that he makes, and which, of course, is made many other times in the New Testament, is that the hope of the Christian is not a beautiful dream, or a wishful thought, but something solid which rests upon the changelessness of God himself. It is, as he says here, "an utterly reliable anchor for our souls." We too need to be reminded of this – that ultimately our hope rests not on our feelings, or lack of them, but upon the utter reliability of God.

A GOSPEL OF HOPE   Hope – 4

AS YOU live this new life, we pray that you will be strengthened from God's boundless resources, so that you will find yourselves able to pass through any experience and endure it with joy. You will even be able to thank God in the midst of pain and distress because you are privileged to share the lot of those who are living in the light. For we must never forget that he rescued us from the power of darkness, and re-established us in the kingdom of his beloved Son. For it is by his Son alone that we have been redeemed and have had our sins forgiven.

I myself have been made a minister of this same gospel, and though it is true at this moment that I am suffering on behalf of you who have heard the gospel, yet I am far from sorry about it. Indeed, I am glad, because it gives me a chance to complete in my own sufferings something of the untold pains which Christ suffers on behalf of his body, the

Church. For I am a minister of the Church by divine commission, a commission granted to me for your benefit and for a special purpose: that I might fully declare God's word – that sacred mystery which up till now has been hidden in every age and every generation, but which is now as clear as daylight to those who love God. They are those to whom God has planned to give a vision of the full wonder and splendour of his secret plan for the nations. And this secret is simply this: Christ *in you*! Yes, Christ *in you* bringing with him the hope of all the glorious things to come. (Coloss. 1: *11–27*)

The old life from which Christ has rescued these Colossian Christians was a life of darkness and despair. It was dark because they did not know the true God and his love, and they had no idea of any real point and purpose in living. And it was full of despair since the pagan religions were powerless to make a reconciliation between man and God. And although they could make fine rules for living they could not provide the power to keep the rules.

By contrast, the Christian gospel is full of life and hope. Not only can men know that they are sons of God, fully reconciled to the Father, but they have reliable grounds, real hope, for believing that they can live up to the new way of living because Christ himself now lives within their personalities.

COMONSENSE HOPE

BUT YOU should never lose sight of this fact, dear friends, that time is not the same with the Lord as it is with us – to him a day may be a thousand years, and a thousand years only a day. It is not that he is dilatory about keeping his own promise, as some men seem to think; the fact is that he is very patient towards you. He has no wish that any man should be destroyed. He wishes that all men should come to repent. Yet it remains true that the day of the Lord will come as suddenly and unexpectedly as a thief. In that day the heavens will disappear in a terrific tearing blast, the very elements will disintegrate in heat, and the earth and all that is in it will be burnt up to nothing.

In view of the fact that all these things are to be dissolved, what sort of people ought you to be? Surely men of good and holy character, who live expecting and earnestly longing for the coming of the day of God. True, this day will mean that the heavens will disappear in fire and the elements disintegrate in fearful heat, but our hopes are set not on these but on the new Heavens and the new earth which he has promised us, and in which nothing but good shall live. Because, my dear friends, you have a hope like this before you, I urge you to make certain that such a day would find you at peace with God and man, clean and blameless in his sight. Meanwhile, consider that God's patience is meant to be man's salvation, as our dear brother Paul pointed out in his letter to you written, out of the wisdom God gave him. In that letter, as indeed in all his letters, he referred to these matters. (II Peter 3: *8-16*)

Whether we take these words about the day of the Lord literally or metaphorically, there can be no doubt at all to the Christian that the time will come when God calls a halt to what we call "life". There will come a time when Eternity, as it were, breaks through into time.

It is important, then, as Peter points out here, that we should never rest any lasting hopes upon this temporary and passing world. The early Christians expected the return in power of the Lord Jesus Christ at any time, and consequently trained themselves not to rest their hopes upon this transitory scheme of things. Now whether what is called here the "Day of the Lord" happens in our life-time or a million years from now, we do not know. But we do know that we shall all die, that is, we shall all have to leave this world, which sometimes looks so substantial, and move into the world which is real and permanent. It is not morbid but commonsense to fix our hopes upon God and our eternal home, and refuse to indulge any lasting hopes in this passing world.

OUR REAL HOME   Hope – 6

FOR YOURSELVES I beg you to stick to the original teaching. If you do, you will be living in fellowship with both the Father and the Son. And that means sharing his own life for ever, as he has promised.

It is true that I felt I had to write the above about men who would dearly love to lead you astray. Yet I know that the touch of his Spirit never leaves you, and you don't really need a human teacher. You know that his Spirit teaches you about all things, always telling you the truth and never telling you a lie. So, as he has taught you, live continually in him. Yes, now, little children, remember to live continually in him. So that if he were suddenly to reveal himself we should still know exactly where we stand, and should not have to shrink away from his presence.

You all know that God is really good. You may be just as sure that the man who leads a really good life is a true child of God.

Consider the incredible love that the Father has shown us in allowing us to be called "children of God" – and this is not just what we are called, but what we *are*. Our heredity on the God-ward side is no mere figure of speech – which explains why the world will no more recognise us than it recognised Christ.

Oh, dear children of mine, have you realised it? Here and now we *are* God's children. We don't know what we shall become in the future. We only know that, if reality were to break through, we should reflect his likeness, for we should see him as he really is!

Everyone who has at heart a hope like that keeps himself pure, for he knows how pure Christ is.

(I John 2: *24*–3: *3*)

However strong hope may be it is, of course, not

the same thing as actually possessing what we are hoping for. St. John is concerned here to point out to his "little children", as he calls them, both what they have already got and what a magnificent hope still lies before them.

Provided that they hold closely to true Christian teaching and are willing to be led by the Spirit of God within them, then here and now they are really and truly children of God. But the light and splendour of Eternity is only a hand's-breadth off. At present we are largely blind and deaf and insensitive to reality. And this is not entirely our own fault. But if reality were to break through, then we should see that the things that we hope for are true, far more true than we ever supposed. Our hopes will be in no way disappointed – they will be infinitely exceeded by the magnificence and beauty of God's real world.

The Christian is cut off for the time being to a large extent from his real home, and from the sight of his beloved master. But he holds in his heart like a warm and precious secret the hope that he has been given.

As we face the strains and stresses, the disappointments and frustrations, of this little life, can we not hold in our hearts a glowing hope that will most certainly not be disappointed?

Hope – 7

IF IT were right to have such confidence, I could certainly have it, and if any of these men thinks he has grounds for such confidence I can assure him I have more. I was born from the people of Israel, I was circumcised on the eighth day, I was a member of the tribe of Benjamin, I was in fact a full-blooded Jew. As far as keeping the Law is concerned I was a Pharisee, and you can judge my enthusiasm for the Jewish faith by my active persecution of the Church. As far as the Law's righteousness is concerned, I don't think anyone could have found fault with me. Yet every advantage that I had gained I considered lost for Christ's sake. Yes, and I look upon everything as loss compared with the overwhelming gain of knowing Christ Jesus my Lord. For his sake I did in actual fact suffer the loss of everything, but I considered it useless rubbish compared with being able to win Christ. For now my place is in him, and I am not dependent upon any of the self-achieved righteousness of the Law. God has given me that genuine righteousness which comes from faith in Christ. How changed are my ambitions! Now I long to know Christ and the power shown by his resurrection: now I long to share his sufferings, even to die as he died, so that I may perhaps attain, as he did, the resurrection from the dead. Yet, my brothers, I do not consider myself to have "arrived", spiritually, nor do I consider myself already perfect. But I keep going on, grasping ever more firmly that purpose for which Christ Jesus grasped me. My brothers, I do not consider myself to have fully grasped it even now. But I do concentrate on this: I leave the past behind and with hands outstretched to whatever lies ahead I go straight for the goal – my reward the honour of my high calling by God in Christ Jesus. (Phil. 3: *4–14*)

There is a strong connection between hope and ambition. Indeed, with many people it would be difficult to disentangle their hopes and ambitions! Here, Paul, who was by nature an extremely ambitious man, shows how fundamentally his ambitions have been changed since he came to know Christ. I think we could fairly say now that his life's ambition is transformed into a great hope – a hope that his life may be worthy of his great master and share in his triumph over death.

It is no bad thing to sort out our own ambitions and hopes. For the Christian, what starts as self-centred ambition should be changed into a hope which is both thrilling and humbling – the hope that we may be of some real use to God.

HOPE FOR CHRISTIAN UNITY   Hope – 8

AS GOD'S prisoner, then, I beg you to live lives worthy of your high calling. Accept life with humility and patience, making allowances for each other because you love each other. Make it your aim to be at one in the Spirit, and you will inevitably be at peace with one another. You all belong to one body, of which there is one Spirit, just as you all experienced one calling to one hope. There is one Lord, one faith, one baptism, one God, one Father of us all, who is the one over all, the one working through all and the one living in all.

Naturally there are different gifts and functions; individually grace is given to us in different ways out of the rich diversity of Christ's giving. As the scripture says:

When he ascended on high, he led captivity captive,
And gave gifts unto men.

His "gifts unto men" were varied. Some he made his messengers, some prophets, some preachers of the gospel; to some he gave the power to guide and teach his people. His gifts were made that Christians might be properly equipped for their service, that the whole body might be built up until the time comes when, in the unity of common faith and common knowledge of the Son of God, we arrive at real maturity – that measure of development which is meant by the "the fulness of Christ".

(Ephes. 4: *1–13*)

It is only the very young or the conceited who think that they can do everything! As life goes on we see more and more clearly that different people are called to do different things. This is true in the ordinary world of human affairs, but it is just as true in the spiritual world. Christians often make themselves miserable because they are not able to do what some other Christians can do. Very often the reason is simply that their gifts from God are different.

But, as Paul is at pains to point out here, *together*, each supplying the lack of the other, we could and should work as Christ's body. Differences of opinion and different ways of looking at things will always be with us, but all Christians need to learn afresh that it is *together* that we comprise the body of Christ. No denomination has a monopoly of God's grace. Paul's great hope expressed here is that the whole body, each part recognising the value of the others, may grow together to true maturity. I wonder how far we are helping to make this hope come true?

HOPE OF A FUTURE LIFE — Hope – 9

NOW IF the rising of Christ from the dead is the very heart of our message, how can some of you deny that there is any resurrection? But if there is no such thing as the resurrection of the dead, then Christ was never raised. And if Christ was not raised then neither our preaching nor your faith has any meaning at all. Further, it would mean that we are lying in our witness for God, for we have given our solemn testimony that he did raise up Christ – and that is utterly false if it should be true that the dead do not, in fact, rise again! For if the dead do not rise neither did Christ rise, and if Christ did not rise your faith is futile and your sins have never been forgiven. Moreover, those who have died believing in Christ are utterly dead and gone. Truly, if our hope in Christ were limited to this life only we should, of all mankind, be the most to be pitied!

But the glorious fact is that Christ *did* rise from the dead: he has become the very first to rise of all who sleep the sleep of death. As death entered the world through a man, so has rising from the dead come to us through a man! As members of a sinful race all men die; as members of the Christ of God all men shall be raised to life, each in his proper order, with Christ the very first and after him all who belong to him when he comes.

Then, and not till then, comes the end when Christ, having abolished all other rule, authority and power, hands over the kingdom to God the Father. Christ's reign will and must continue until every enemy has been conquered. The last enemy of all to be destroyed is death itself.

(I Cor. 15: *12-26*)

A very important part of our Christian hope is the hope of triumphing over death. It is easy, indeed it is common to all people of the world, to *hope* that we may survive death. But as I have said before, there is all the difference in the world between a hope with reasonable grounds and a hope which is merely a wishful thought. In plain sober fact, our hope of passing through death to share in God's eternal life rests upon Christ's own demonstration with the enemy, his rising from the dead. It is the crux of the Christian faith. For if Christ had never risen, his own claims would have been proved false, and his own promise to be personally the "Resurrection and the Life" would be no more than fine-sounding words.

Sooner or later we have to make up our minds whether we accept as sober historical fact the resurrection of Christ from the dead. If you think about it, we have no other solid ground for hope in our own personal resurrection.

What launched the Christian Church, with all its fire and energy and courage, upon a pagan world? Was it hysteria? Hallucination? Some ingenious swindle? Would men live and die for any of these things? But suppose the resurrection did really happen. Not only is the faith of the early Church accounted for, but we ourselves have a sure and certain hope of entering the new life with him.

OUR GREAT HOPE　　　　　　　　　　　Hope – 10

REMEMBER ALWAYS, as the centre of everything, Jesus Christ, a descendant of David, yet raised by God from the dead according to my gospel. For preaching this I am having to endure being chained in prison as if I were some sort of criminal. But they cannot chain the Word of God, and I can endure all these things for the sake of those whom God is calling, so that they too may receive the salvation of Christ Jesus, and its complement of glory after the world of time. I rely on this saying: *If we died with him we shall also live with him: if we suffer with him we shall also reign with him. If we deny him he will also deny us: yet if we are faithless he always remains faithful. He cannot deny his own nature.*

Remind your people of things like this, and tell them as before God not to fight wordy battles, which help no one and may undermine the faith of some who hear them.

For yourself, concentrate on winning God's approval, on being a workman with nothing to be ashamed of, and who knows how to use the word of truth to the best advantage. But steer clear of these un-Christian babblings, which in practice lead further and further away from Christian living. For their teachings are as dangerous as blood-poisoning to the body, and spread like sepsis from a wound. (II Tim. 2: *8–17*)

God's solid foundation still stands, however, with this double inscription: *"The Lord knows those who belong to him"* and *"Let every true Christian have no dealings with evil"*.

We are all familiar with the saying "Crime does not pay". But it must often have appeared in the early days of our Faith that Christianity did not pay! Paul himself suffered fifty times what you and I are ever likely to have to suffer in a life-time, and we know that the early Christians suffered all sorts of torture and persecution for the sake of their faith. Yet their hopes were fixed beyond this passing world, and the best of them did not greatly care what this little life might bring to them because they were so sure of their standing in Eternity.

Quite apart from persecution and martyrdom, which is not very likely to come our way, the devil is always likely to suggest to us that "Christianity does not pay". We could have a better time, we could make more money, we could be freer from responsibilities, if we were not attempting to follow in the footsteps of Jesus Christ. I think we have to say quite firmly to ourselves that Christianity does not by any means always pay in the here-and-now. Christians often have to bear burdens and share sorrows, and sometimes endure ridicule, in a way that the cheerful agnostic knows nothing about. But, as Paul rightly says, "If we suffer with him, we shall also reign with him." This is our great hope.

IV
LOVE

The First and Great Commandment

TO LOVE God with the whole of our personalities and powers is, according to the words of Christ recorded in Matthew 22: *38*, the "first and great commandment". Yet among the thousands of people outside the ranks of the Church there would be very few who could be found to agree with him. "Be a decent chap and don't worry your head too much about God" – this is the working philosophy of a good many people.

Those of us who profess and call ourselves Christians are committed to accept Christ's authority, though not unthinkingly; and when we come to look behind what appear at first to be arbitrary commands, we find that invariably he had good reasons for the principles he laid down. So it is here. Let us consider three of the many reasons why Christ insisted that whole-hearted love of God was the primary and most important principle of human life.

The Only Source of True "Values"

Unless we believe in God and love him, the qualities we value, the things we call "good" or "bad", are purely a matter of personal opinion. Your "good" may be my "bad" and vice versa. This is by no means clear to the average Englishman today; he probably thinks that we regard certain lines of conduct as good or bad by the light of nature. But this is not really so – it only seems like it because this country of ours has had centuries of Christian tradition. Our ways of living and thinking are permeated, even for the Godless, by Christian ideals. Christians, though comparatively few in number, have an influence on national thought and conscience out of all proportion to their numerical strength; and even today a very large part of our tradition of behaviour is nothing less than the fruit of Christian ideals having percolated almost imperceptibly into our habits of thinking.

You may still think that I am exaggerating, and that these "values" of right and wrong would exist in any case. Perhaps I can make myself plainer if I give you two pointers to the truth about the matter.

Consider first the moral atmosphere of a country where there is no Christian tradition. Some of us have lived in such countries, and others have visited them. I know from the letters I have myself received from young people, abroad on national service, just how big a shock it is to discover that the moral values that everyone takes for granted at home are by no means universally acknowledged. Take the very simple virtue of kindness to animals. We are universally agreed, in this country, that it is a good thing to be kind to animals, and that even if we do not especially like them, we should never deliberately hurt an animal. But in a non-Christian country, Egypt for example, to be kind to animals is by no means the traditional taken-for-granted attitude. Again, we almost automatically think it right to care for the poor, the weak, the sick and the aged; but there are several non-Christian countries where such people are shamefully neglected, and no one seems to think it wrong. No, the justice, the fair-play, the mercy and tolerance that we think are self-evident virtues, are by no means commonly found in countries where the true God is unknown or disregarded.

A further instance. In the sphere of international politics we take it for granted that other countries will hold the same moral values as we do. But, alas, in countries where the place of God is taken by the State we do not find that their moral conceptions are by any means the same as the ones to which we are accustomed. For example, we know very well that it is right and that it is our duty to feed the hungry of any nation, to care for refugees, and strictly to respect the integrity of countries smaller than our own. But when we come into contact with a country which is its own god, we find, rather to our horror, that what we took for granted is by no means accepted by a non-Christian community. The justice and fair-play that we consider should be accorded to small and weak nations – and even to a defeated enemy – may be considered foolishly quixotic by a nation which does not acknowledge the first and great commandment.

Again, to return to the Christian "atmosphere" of our own land. It exists because there have been many, and still are quite a number of people, who do love God, but we can already begin to trace a decline in moral standards where the Christian tradition is beginning to lose its hold. In our Sunday Schools, for example, you will find a few children who have been brought up with at least some Christian teaching, but the majority have not even been taught in their homes to say their prayers – and have certainly not been trained in the Christian way of living or to have Christian ideals. These are the children of parents who have little or no religious faith, and whose parents before them likewise lacked any positive Christian belief or practice. Thus, when the first and great commandment has been neglected or disobeyed for two or three generations, there is a most marked falling off in moral standards, and this decline is taking place all over the country.

"Be a decent chap and don't worry too much about God" is all very well, but the time comes when God has been so neglected that people no longer want to behave like "decent chaps". And what are you to do then? No, the first and great commandment is extremely important because without it you are bound to get a sudden, or gradual, decline in moral values. Nor is that all, for the place in the human heart that should be occupied by God can be very easily filled with a false god by unscrupulous people – which is the fate that befell the youth of Nazi Germany.

The Only Ground for obeying the Second Commandment

It is comparatively easy for us to love those "neighbours" who are nice and friendly towards us. It is easy to love the attractive and charming personalities of our friends. But Christ made it quite clear that loving our "neighbour" did not stop at loving our particular circle, but loving all those with whom life brought us into contact.

You will remember his semi-humorous comment on those who thought that to love their particular friends was enough – "Do not even the publicans the same?" We might paraphrase that – "Aren't even the tax-collectors nice to their pals?" No, if there is ever to be a happy and peaceful world we have all of us got to learn to understand and to love the difficult, the exasperating, and the unlovable – and that is a superhuman task.

I use the word "superhuman" deliberately, for by ourselves, without the inspiration that comes from loving God, it is plainly impossible for us to love, in the sense that Christ uses the word, our fellow men.

A clergyman probably realises this far more acutely than the average layman. There are many departments of life where obviously you possess more knowledge and experience than I do; but in this matter of living in love and charity with all kinds of people the parson has to know a good deal. Forgive my plain speaking, but is it not true that if you find someone who is "difficult" or conceited or annoying, it is quite the easiest thing in the world for you simply to withdraw yourself and make friends with just those with whom you get on? But such a course is not open to me. I have to learn to understand and work with all kinds of different temperaments and outlooks, and in consequence I get a unique opportunity of seeing just how difficult is Christ's second commandment – to love other people as we love ourselves.

Frankly, I see no prospect of our even wanting to obey the second commandment seriously until we have begun to obey the first. We don't really see other men and women as our brothers and sisters simply by talking airily about the brotherhood of man. We only see them as such when we begin to get a vision of God the Father. It is so fatally easy to talk high-falutin hot air about all the world being "one big family", and yet fail to "get on" with the members of our own families, or with those who live next door, or in the flat above us. In sober fact, men do not really love their fellows, except their own particular friends, until they have seriously begun to love God. It is only then that we learn to drop the destructive attitude of hatred and contempt and criticism, and begin to adopt the constructive attitude of Christian love. So, then, the second reason for the command to love God being "the first and great commandment" is that we don't really keep the second until we have obeyed the first.

The Only Safeguard against State-worship

More and more in these modern days, in many countries besides our own, men are being called to give their loyalty to the State. Though it is not my duty to talk politics, thank goodness, I must point out what an absurd, and dangerous, thing this exaltation of the State can be. It is absurd because the State has no *real* existence, It is at best only a convenient name for the combined interests of other people. It doesn't, for example, remain the same even for twenty-four hours! Last night more than a hundred people died throughout this country, and possibly the same number was born. In quite a small number of years, therefore, the "State" has entirely changed its personnel, and it cannot claim to have any real, that is, permanent existence. God, however, really does exist and human beings who are linked to him also really exist, because he has promised that those who live according to his will, will share in his timeless existence.

The Church also has a real existence, for it is permanent and by no means limited to this life – indeed, it is the only society to which we may belong whose membership does not cease at death. But to exalt the State as though it could claim the highest loyalties of man, whose home is eternity, is simply grotesque. It is, in fact, the blasphemy which naturally follows the replacement of the first and great commandment by the second.

The interests of other people are indeed important, but to exalt them to the position of God is dangerous – both because such State-worship tends to extinguish the value of the individual (whom God has made individual), and because it attempts to claim a loyalty which cannot be given to anyone or anything but God without loss of liberty.

The Secret of Happiness

There may, of course, be those who resent this great principle being represented as a command. "How can I love to order?" they might say. "Surely you can't be made to love just by being given a command." I appreciate this, but if you will forget the words "command" and "commandment" for a moment you will see what Christ is really saying. He states quite plainly that there are two unalterable principles for happy, harmonious, satisfying human living. The first and most important is to set your affections and loyalties upon the very highest, upon the supreme mind and heart behind the whole scheme of things. The second is to bestow upon other people that understanding and tolerant love that we so readily accord ourselves.

It is quite true that we cannot love "to order", but we have the power to choose where we shall bestow our affections and loyalties. We can choose whether we turn them in upon ourselves, whether we give them to false impermanent gods of our own making; or whether we deliberately set them upon the very highest that we know. Christ knew the secret of happy, effectual and harmonious living, both for individuals and for nations, and it is simply this – to love God first with the whole of our powers and personalities, and then to extend to others the deep-seated love we have for ourselves. But the order of these two principles cannot be reversed: to love God with heart and soul and mind and strength remains the first and great commandment.

THE WAY OF LOVE Love – 1

WHEN THE Pharisees heard that he had silenced the Sadducees they came up to him in a body, and one of them, an expert in the Law, put this test-question: "Master, what are we to consider the Law's greatest commandment?"

Jesus answered him, "'Thou shalt love the Lord thy God with all thy heart, and with all thy soul and with all thy mind.' This is the first and great commandment. And there is a second like it: 'Thou shalt love thy neighbour as thyself.' The whole of the Law and the Prophets depends on these two commandments." (Matthew 22: *34–40*)

Keep out of debt altogether, except that perpetual debt of love which we owe one another. The man who loves his neighbour has obeyed the whole Law in regard to his neighbour. For the commandments, "Thou shalt not commit adultery", "Thou shalt not kill", "Thou shalt not steal", "Thou shalt not covet" and all other commandments are summed up in this one saying: "Thou shalt love thy neighbour as thyself." Love hurts nobody: therefore love is the answer to the Law's commands.
(Romans 13: *8–10*)

For the Jews in Christ's time, religion had become a very complicated business, full of rules and regulations. Indeed, it had become so complex that a great many people could not hope to fulfil all the Law's detailed instructions. We are not therefore surprised to find somebody asking Jesus what he considered was the most important commandment. In his reply Jesus goes right to the very heart and core of the matter: all religion and all morality depend quite simply on a man's loving God with the whole of his personality and loving his neighbour with the same love which he naturally has for himself.

Paul, who had himself been a Pharisee, and knew

the Law inside out, tells his Roman readers exactly the same thing. The answer to all moral and religious demands lies not in a tight-lipped, determined effort, but in a heart opened by the love of God and prepared to give love to other people.

Whatever denomination we may belong to, there are times when it is very good for us to go back to the heart of the matter. All our creeds, all our formulas, all our safeguards for the truth, are worth nothing at all unless we fulfil the basic commands to love God, and to love our neighbours as ourselves.

There are people who think that the two commandments of Jesus are somehow a watering-down of the ten commandments of Moses. If they think that, then they plainly have not tried the way of Christ, which is the way of love. If we follow that way seriously, we shall find it far surpasses the demands of Moses' Law. The ten commandments may produce law-abiding people, but the Law of Christ produces sons and daughters of God.

Love – 2

TO YOU whom I love I say, let us go on loving one another, for love comes from God. Every man who truly loves God is God's son and has some knowledge of him But the man who does not love cannot know him at all, for God is love.

To us, the greatest demonstration of God's love

for us has been his sending his only Son into the world to give us life through him. We see real love, not in the fact that we loved God, but that he loved us and sent his Son to make personal atonement for our sins. If God loved us as much as that, surely we, in our turn, should love each other!

It is true that no human being has ever had a direct vision of God. Yet if we love each other God does actually live within us, and his love grows in us towards perfection. And, as I wrote above, the guarantee of our living in him and his living in us is the share of his own Spirit which he gives us.

We ourselves are eye-witnesses able and willing to testify to the fact that the Father did send the Son to save the world. Everyone who acknowledges that Jesus is the Son of God finds that God lives in him, and he lives in God. So have we come to know and trust the love God has for us. God *is* love, and the man whose life is lived in love does, in fact, live in God, and God does, in fact, live in him. So our love for him grows more and more, filling us with complete confidence for the day when he shall judge all men – for we realise that our life in this world is actually his life lived in us. Love contains no fear – indeed fully-developed love expels every particle of fear, for fear always contains some of the torture of feeling guilty. This means that the man who lives in fear has not yet had his love perfected.

Yes, we love him because he first loved us. If a man says, "I love God" and hates his brother he is a liar. For if he does not love the brother before his eyes how can he love the one beyond his sight? And in any case it is his explicit command that the one who loves God must love his brother too.

(I John 4: *7–21*)

It is apparently part of God's plan that we should show our love for him, whom we have never seen, by loving those about us whom we can see. Of course this is not easy, for people are by no means always lovable. It is a healthy thing to reflect that just as some people annoy us, so we probably annoy somebody else! Indeed it is more than probable that we don't appear particularly lovable to God himself. Yet he loves us, and we are called to love our fellowmen in the same way as he loves us. This is a supernatural task, but God will be with us and in us to make it possible.

THE BEST KIND OF LOVE   Love – 3

THIS PASSAGE really needs no comment. It simply underlines what we all know in our hearts to be true – that the best kind of life is the life lived in love for God and our fellows:

> The man who lives a consistently good life is a good man, as surely as God is good. But the man whose life is habitually sinful is spiritually a son of the devil, for the devil is behind all sin, as he always has been. Now the Son of God came to earth with the express purpose of liquidating the devil's activities. The man who is really God's son does not practise sin, for God's nature is in him, for good, and such a heredity is incapable of sin.
> Here we have a clear indication as to who are the

children of God and who are the children of the devil. The man who does not lead a good life is no son of God, nor is the man who fails to love his brother. For the original command, as you know, is that we should love one another. We are none of us to have the spirit of Cain, who was a son of the devil and murdered his brother. Have you realised his motive? It was just because he realised the goodness of his brother's life and the rottenness of his own. Don't be surprised, therefore, if the world hates you.

We know that we have crossed the frontier from death to life because we do love our brothers. The man without love for his brother is living in death already. The man who actively hates his brother is a potential murderer, and you will readily see that the eternal life of God cannot live in the heart of a murderer.

We know and, to some extent realise, the love of God for us because Christ expressed it in laying down his life for us. We must in turn express our love by laying down our lives for those who are our brothers. But as for the well-to-do man who sees his brother in want but shuts his eyes – and his heart – how could anyone believe that the love of God lives in him? My children, let us love not merely in theory or in words – let us love in sincerity and in practice!

If we live like this, we shall know that we are children of the truth and can reassure ourselves in the sight of God, even if our hearts make us feel guilty. For God is infinitely greater than our hearts, and he knows everything. And if, dear friends of mine, when we realise this our hearts no longer accuse us, we may have the utmost confidence in

God's presence. We receive whatever we ask for, because we are obeying his orders and following his plans. His orders are that we should put our trust in the name of his Son, Jesus Christ, and love one another – as we used to hear him say in person.

The man who does obey God's commands lives in God and God lives in him, and the guarantee of his presence within us is the Spirit he has given us.

(I John 3: *7–24*)

NEGATIVE AND POSITIVE VIRTUE   Love – 4

THERE WAS once a rich man who used to dress in purple and fine linen and lead a life of daily luxury. And there was a poor man called Lazarus who was put down at his gate. He was covered with sores. He used to long to be fed with the scraps from the rich man's table. Yes, and the dogs used to come and lick his sores. Well, it happened that the poor man died, and was carried by the angels into Abraham's bosom. The rich man also died and was buried. And from among the dead he looked up and saw Abraham a long way away, and Lazarus in his arms. "Father Abraham!", he cried out, "Please pity me. Send Lazarus to dip the tip of his finger in water and cool my tongue, for I am in agony in these flames." But Abraham replied, "Remember, my son, that you used to get the good things in your lifetime, while Lazarus suffered the bad. Now he is being comforted here while you are in agony. And besides this, a great chasm has been set between you and us, so that those who want to go to you from this side cannot do so, and people cannot come to us from your side." At this he said, "Then I beg you to send him to my father's house' for I have five brothers. He could warn them about all this and prevent their coming to this place of torture." But Abraham said, "They have Moses and the prophets: they can listen to them." "Ah no, father Abraham," he said, "if only someone went to them from the dead, they would change completely." But Abraham told him, "If they will not listen to Moses and the prophets, they would not be convinced even if somebody were to rise from the dead." (Luke 16: *19–31*)

People frequently say, especially as they are drawing near to the end of their lives, "I never did anyone any harm." That may be true, but it is a very negative sort of virtue. It would be appropriate to ask, "All right, but what sort of *good* did you do to people?" To fail to do good to people when we have opportunity is just as sinful in the eyes of God as actively doing them harm.

This memorable story is used by Jesus to bring out this point. As far as we know the rich man who lived in such luxury was not an evil-living man at all, according to ordinary standards, but in God's sight he failed completely, because he failed in love. He did nothing positive for the unhappy beggar who lived at his very gate.

We need to beware of a life of negative virtue, and in the light of this rather alarming parable to ask ourselves not merely, "Am I doing anyone any harm?" but also "Am I doing all the good I can?" In other words, "Am I really living the life of love to which I am called?"

RELIGION AND LIFE   Love – 5

THEN ONE of the experts in the Law stood up to test him and said,

"Master, what must I do to be sure of eternal life?"

"What does the Law say and what has your reading taught you?" asked Jesus.

"The Law says, Thou shalt love the Lord thy God with all thy heart and with all thy soul and with all thy strength and with all thy mind – and thy neighbour as thyself," he replied.

"Quite right," said Jesus. "Do that and you will live."

But the man, wanting to justify himself, continued,

"But who is my neighbour?"

And Jesus gave him the following reply:

"A man was once on his way down from Jerusalem to Jericho. He fell into the hands of bandits who stripped off his clothes, beat him up, and left him half dead. It so happened that a priest was going down that road, and when he saw him, he passed by on the other side. A Levite also came on the scene and when he saw him, he too passed by on the other side. But then a Samaritan traveller came along to the place where the man was lying, and at the sight of him he was touched with pity. He went across to him and bandaged his wounds, pouring on oil and wine. Then he put him on his own mule, brought him to an inn, and did what he could for him. Next day he took out ten shillings and gave it to the inn-keeper with the words, 'Look after him, will you? I will pay you back anything more than this that you spend, when I come through here on my return.' Which of these three seems to you to have been a neighbour to the bandits' victim?"

"The man who gave him practical sympathy," he replied.

"Then you go and give the same," replied Jesus.
(Luke 10: *25-37*)

If we read the Gospels with open minds, one of the things which is most striking about the teaching of Christ is his insistence on the connection between religion and life. He will not allow them to exist in two separate compartments. Love for God must be expressed in love for other people.

We don't know much about this "expert in the Law", but he was obviously one of those tidy-minded people who liked to have everything straight in his mind. He wanted to know just how far his obligations should extend. I don't suppose the parable which we call "The Parable of the Good Samaritan", which Jesus told him by way of reply to his question, was much of a comfort. At a guess I should say he expected some religious answer to his question, which he could neatly docket away in his mind and perform without much effort. But Jesus will not allow this kind of thing. He requires a man to learn to give himself even at the cost of his own comfort and convenience. No one can take refuge from the demands of Jesus in "religion". It is a life of practical outgoing love that he requires of us.

THE HUMILITY OF LOVE   Love – 6

NOW IF your experience of Christ's encouragement and love means anything to you, if you have known something of the fellowship of his Spirit, and all that it means in kindness and deep sympathy, do make my best hopes for you come true! Live together in harmony, live together in love, as though you had only one mind and one spirit between you. Never act from motives of rivalry or personal vanity, but in humility think more of each other than you do of yourselves. None of you should think only of his own affairs, but should learn to see things from other people's point of view.

Let Christ Jesus be your example as to what your attitude should be. For he, who had always been God by nature, did not cling to his prerogatives as God's equal, but stripped himself of all privilege by consenting to be a slave by nature and being born as mortal man. And, having become man, he humbled himself by living a life of utter obedience, even to the extent of dying, *and the death he died was the death of a common criminal*. That is why God has now lifted him so high, and has given him the name beyond all names, so that at the name of Jesus "every knee shall bow", whether in Heaven or earth or under the earth. And that is why, in the end, "every tongue shall confess" that Jesus Christ is the Lord, to the glory of God the Father.

So then, my dearest friends, as you have always followed my advice – and that not only when I was present to give it – so now that I am far away be keener than ever to work out the salvation that God has given you with a proper sense of awe and responsibility. For it is God who is at work within you, giving you the will and the power to achieve his purpose.

Do all you have to do without grumbling or arguing, so that you may be God's children, blameless, sincere and wholesome, living in a warped and diseased world, and shining there like lights in a dark place For you hold in your hands the very word of life. (Phil. 2: *1–16*)

I don't know whether you've noticed it, but pride and fear go together very often in life, and so do love and humility. Many people complain of fears, yet it often turns out on calm analysis that their fears were rooted in pride. If their pride were dissolved most of their fears would disappear.

The only solvent that I know for dissolving pride is to receive more and more of the love of God and to give more and more love to other people. In this passage Paul is recommending his readers to consider again the incredible humility and love of Christ's action in becoming man. When the way of love, which is what we are called to as Christians, challenges our pride, it is a good thing to look again at the awe-inspiring humility of Christ. Pride may be humiliated by all sorts of things, but it is only melted away by sheer practical humble love.

IN CLOSE TOUCH WITH GOD   Love – 7

"IF YOU really love me, you will keep the commandments I have given you and I shall ask the Father to give you someone else to stand by you, to be with you always. I mean the Spirit of truth, whom the world cannot accept, for it can neither see nor recognise that Spirit. But you recognise him, for he is with you now and will be in your hearts. I am not going to leave you alone in the world – I am coming to you. In a very little while, the world will see me no more but you will see me, because I am really alive and you will be alive, too. When that day comes, you will realise that I am in my Father, that you are in me, and I am in you.

"Every man who knows my commandments and obeys them is the man who really loves me, and the man who really loves me will himself be loved by my Father, and I too will love him and make myself known to him."

Then Judas (not Iscariot) said, "Lord, how is it that you are going to make yourself known to us but not to the world?" And to this Jesus replied, "When a man loves me, he follows my teaching. Then my Father will love him, and we will come to that man and make our home within him. The man who does not really love me will not follow my teaching. Indeed, what you are hearing from me now is not really my saying, but comes from the Father who sent me.

"I have said all this while I am still with you. But the one who is coming to stand by you, the Holy Spirit whom the Father will send in my name, will be your teacher and will bring to your minds all that I have said to you.

"I leave behind with you – peace; I give you my own peace and my gift is nothing like the peace of this world. You must not be distressed and you must not be daunted." (John 14: *15-27*)

People have sometimes said to me that the most *real* parts of their lives are the times when they have really given themselves in love. I have had this sort of remark made to me even by people without any particular religious faith. For myself I don't think it is at all surprising, for if God is love, and if he is not far from any one of us, then when we act in love, it seems quite reasonable to suppose that we are touching, however distantly, the life of God himself.

But we need not be content with a vague feeling that the life of love is more real and satisfying than any other kind of living. In these immensely valuable words of Jesus Christ, we see how we may be in close touch with God through Christ, and loving our fellow-men for Christ's sake. The more we love, the more we co-operate with the loving purpose of God, the more real God will become to us.

To love God and our fellow-men for Christ's sake will bring us both the sense of God's reality and the peace of Christ in our hearts.

LIVING TOGETHER IN LOVE   Love – 8

MEN HAVE different gifts, but it is the same Spirit who gives them. There are different ways of serving God, but it is the same Lord who is served. God works through different men in different ways, but it is the same God who achieves his purposes through them all. Each man is given his gift by the Spirit that he may make the most of it.

One man's gift by the Spirit is to speak with wisdom, another's to speak with knowledge. The same Spirit gives to another man faith, to another the ability to heal, to another the power to do great deeds. The same Spirit gives to another man the gift of preaching the word of God, to another the ability to discriminate in spiritual matters, to another speech in different tongues and to yet another the power to interpret the tongues. Behind all these gifts is the operation of the same Spirit, who distributes to each individual man, as he wills.

As the human body, which has many parts, is a unity, and those parts, despite their multiplicity, constitute one single body, so it is with Christ. For we were all baptised by the Spirit into one body, whether we were Jews, Greeks, slaves or free men, and we have all had experience of the same Spirit.

Now the body is not one member but many. If the foot should say, "Because I am not a hand I don't belong to the body", does that alter the fact that the foot *is* a part of the body? Or if the ear should say, "Because I am not an eye I don't belong to the body", does that mean that the ear really is no part of the body? After all, if the body were all one eye, for example, where would be the sense of hearing? Or if it were all one ear, where would be the sense of smell? But God has arranged all the parts in the one body, according to his design. For if everything were concentrated in one part, how could there be a body at all? The fact is there are many parts, but only one body. So that the eye cannot say to the hand, "I don't need you!" nor, again, can the head say to the feet, "I don't need you!" On the contrary, those parts of the body which have no obvious function are the more essential to health; and to those parts of the body which seem to us to be less deserving of notice we have to allow the highest honour of function.

Now you are together the body of Christ, and individually you are members of him.

(I Cor. 12: *4–27*)

One of the things which prevents human beings living together in love is that people don't always recognise how different we are one from another. In this famous passage Paul is making clear the fact that God has given different gifts to different people, and it is only *together* that they make up one body. We need to beware of the secret thought, "If everyone were like me, what a much better world it would be" – or of looking down on somebody else just because he or she has not got our particular gifts. We need to use our sense of humour, our imagination and our common sense if we are to learn to live together in love.

GENUINE LOVE   Love – 9

SO MAY God our Father himself and our Lord Jesus guide our steps to you. May the Lord give you the same increasing and overflowing love for each other and towards all men as we have towards you. May he establish you, holy and blameless in heart and soul, before God, the Father of us all, when our Lord Jesus comes with all who belong to him. To sum up, my brothers, we beg and pray you by the Lord Jesus, that you continue to learn more and more of the life that pleases God, the sort of life we told you about before. You will remember the instructions we gave you then in the name of the Lord Jesus. God's plan is to make you holy, and that entails first of all a clean cut with sexual immorality. Every one of you should learn to control his body, keeping it pure and treating it with respect, and never regarding it as an instrument for self-gratification, as do pagans with no knowledge of God. You cannot break this rule without in some way cheating your fellow-men. And you must remember that God will punish all who do offend in this matter, and we have warned you how we have seen this work out in our experience of life. The calling of God is not to impurity but to the most thorough purity, and anyone who makes light of the matter is not making light of a man's ruling but of God's command. It is not for nothing that the Spirit God gives us is called the *Holy* Spirit.

Next, as regards brotherly love, you don't need any written instructions. God himself is teaching you to love each other, and you are already extending your love to all the Macedonians. Yet we urge you to have more and more of this love, and to make it your ambition to have no ambition! Be busy with your own affairs and do your work yourselves. The result will be a reputation for honesty in the world outside and an honourable independence.

(I Thess. 3: *11*–4: *12*)

As every Christian knows there is a lot which goes by the name of love nowadays which is not really love at all. However wonderful and glamorous a passion may be, if it is going to hurt someone else, even indirectly, it cannot be genuine love – the sort of love which comes from God who is love. In this passage, then, Paul is recommending proper control of our God-given instincts and desires, and it might well be taken to heart by people who misuse the word "love" for their own pleasure.

It is no part of the Christian faith to deny the beauty, the romance and even the glamour of true love. But the sort of love which a Christian uses and develops goes far beyond these things. By the Spirit of God within him he is really concerned for the welfare of others. The ways in which he expresses his love will always be those which mean the good, and never the harm, of other people.

THE MOST IMPORTANT THING IN THE WORLD Love – 10

IF I speak with the eloquence of men and of angels, but have no love, I become no more than blaring brass or crashing cymbal. If I have the gift of foretelling the future and hold in my mind not only all human knowledge but the very secrets of God, and if I also have that absolute faith which can move mountains, but have no love, I amount to nothing at all. If I dispose of all that I possess, yes, even if I give my own body to be burned, but have no love, I achieve precisely nothing.

This love of which I speak is slow to lose patience – it looks for a way of being constructive. It is not possessive: it is neither anxious to impress nor does it cherish inflated ideas of its own importance.

Love has good manners and does not pursue selfish advantage. It is not touchy. It does not keep account of evil or gloat over the wickedness of other people. On the contrary, it is glad with all good men when truth prevails.

Love knows no limit to its endurance, no end to its trust, no fading of its hope; it can outlast anything. It is, in fact, the one thing that still stands when all else has fallen.

For if there are prophecies they will be fulfilled and done with, if there are "tongues" the need for them will disappear, if there is knowledge it will be swallowed up in truth. For our knowledge is always incomplete and our prophecy is always incomplete, and when the complete comes, that is the end of the incomplete.

When I was a little child I talked and felt and

thought like a little child. Now that I am a man my childish speech and feeling and thought have no further significance for me.

At present we are men looking at puzzling reflections in a mirror. The time will come when we shall see reality whole and face to face! At present all I know is a little fraction of the truth, but the time will come when I shall know it as fully as God now knows me!

In this life we have three great lasting qualities – faith, hope and love. But the greatest of them is love. (I Cor. 13: *1–13*)

Paul was a man of enormous energy, drive and courage. There must be very few men indeed who accomplished what he accomplished in one lifetime. Yet after years of Christian work he has become convinced that the most important thing in the world is love. Without this vital quality all his efforts in the long run accomplish nothing at all. The things which we as Christians can see as part of the purpose of God are those things which we did in the spirit of love. It is when we love that, under God, we succeed. And it is when we fail to love that we fail completely.

V

THE CHRISTIAN YEAR

1. THE MEANING OF ADVENT

BY FAR the most important and significant event in the whole course of human history will be celebrated, with or without understanding, at the end of this season of Advent. The towering miracle of God's visit to this planet on which we live will be glossed over, brushed aside or rendered impotent by over-familiarity. Even by the Christian the full weight of the event is not always appreciated. His faith is in Jesus Christ – he believes with all his heart that that man, who lived and died and rose again in Palestine, was truly the Son of God. He may have, in addition, some working experience that the man Jesus is still alive, and yet be largely unaware of the intense meaning of what he believes.

Does he, for instance, as he daily treads the surface of this planet, reflect with confidence that "my God has been here, here on this earth"? Does he keep his faith wrapped in a napkin as a thing precious and apart; or does he allow every discovery of the truth to enlarge his conception of the God behind this immensely complex universe? And does he then marvel and adore the infinite wisdom and power which could descend to human stature? We rejoice in the fact that God has actually been here – and that is one half of the meaning of Advent.

But there is another half. The eleven, who had had six weeks' experience of the risen Christ, were told after he had finally left their sight, that "this same Jesus shall so come in like manner as ye have seen him go".

As a translator of the New Testament I find in it no support whatever for the belief that one day all evil will be eradicated from the earth, all problems solved, and health and wealth be every man's portion! Even among some Christians such a belief is quite commonly held, so that the "second advent" of Christ is no more and no less than the infinite number of "comings" of Christ into men's minds. Of course, no one would deny that there are millions of such "comings" every year – but that is not what the Christian Church believes by the second advent of Christ; and it is most emphatically not what any writer of the New Testament ever meant in foretelling his second coming.

The New Testament is indeed a book full of hope, but we may search it in vain for any vague humanist optimism. The second coming of Christ, the second irruption of eternity into time, will be immediate, violent, and conclusive. The human experiment is to end, illusion will give way to reality, the temporary disappear before the permanent, and the king will be seen for who he is. The thief in the night, the lightning flash, the sound of the last trumpet, the voice of God's archangel – these may all be picture-language, but they are pictures of something sudden, catastrophic, and decisive. By no stretch of the imagination do they describe a gradual process.

I believe that the atheistic-scientific-humanist point of view, which affects so much thinking today, is, despite its apparent humanitarianism, both misleading and cruel. In appearance it may resemble Christianity in that it would encourage tolerance, love, understanding, and the amelioration of human conditions. But at heart it is cruel, because it teaches that this life is the only life, that men have no place prepared for them in eternity, and that the only realities are those which they can appreciate in their present temporary habitation. Hence the current hysterical preoccupation with physical security, particularly in relation to the hydrogen-bomb, which infects the lives of many professing Christians. When, we may well ask, have Christians been promised physical security? In the early Church it is evident that they did not even expect it! Their security, their true life, was rooted in God; and neither the daily insecurities of the decaying Roman Empire, nor the organised persecution which followed later, could affect their basic confidence.

In my judgement, the description which Christ gave of the days that were to come before his return is more accurately reproduced in this fear-ridden age than ever before in the course of human history. Of course we do not know the times and the seasons, but at least we can refuse to be deceived by the current obsession for physical security in the here-and-now. While we continue to pray and work for the spread of the kingdom in this transitory world, we know that its centre of gravity is not here at all. When God decides that the human experiment has gone on long enough, yes, even in the midst of what appears to us confusion and incompleteness, Christ will come again.

This is what the New Testament teaches. This is the message of Advent. It is for us to be alert, vigilant and industrious, so that his coming will not be a terror but an overwhelming joy.

2. PREPARING FOR CHRISTMAS

ACCORDING TO the old saying, familiarity breeds contempt. Of course this is not always true! In particular, it is often not true of people with whom we are familiar. Indeed, with the best kind of friends the more we know them the more we grow to love and respect them. It is only the people who are superficial and at heart unreal who let us down when we grow familiar with them. It is then that our previous admiration can easily turn into contempt.

But the old saying was not necessarily intended to apply only to human relationships. There are situations where human beings are at first filled with awe, and then as they grow more and more familiar with them they experience first indifference, and then contempt. The "spider-man", who works on scaffolding hundreds of feet above the ground, has to be on his guard against this over-familiarity. The man who works with high-voltage electricity must also beware of becoming contemptuous of his danger. And anyone who knows the sea will say to you in effect, "By all means love the sea, but never lose your respect for it." Whenever familiarity breeds contempt there is potential danger.

The particular danger which faces us as Christmas approaches is unlikely to be contempt for the sacred season, but nevertheless our familiarity with it may easily produce in us a kind of indifference. The true wonder and mystery may leave us unmoved; familiarity may easily blind us to the shining fact which lies at the heart of Christmas-tide. We are all aware of the commercialisation of Christmas; we can hardly help being involved in the frantic business of buying and sending gifts and cards. We shall without doubt enjoy the carols, the decorations, the feasting and jollification, the presents, the parties, the dancing and the general atmosphere of goodwill which almost magically permeates the days of Christmas. But we may not always see clearly that so much decoration and celebration has been heaped upon the festival that the historic fact upon which all the rejoicing is founded has been almost smothered out of existence.

What we are in fact celebrating is the awe-inspiring humility of God, and no amount of familiarity with the trappings of Christmas should ever blind us to its quiet but explosive significance. For Christians believe that so great is God's love and concern for mankind that he himself became a man. Amid the sparkle and colour and music of the days' celebration we do well to remember that God's insertion of himself into human history was achieved with an almost frightening quietness and humility. There was no advertisement, no publicity, no special privilege; in fact the entry of God into his own world was almost heart-breakingly humble. In sober fact there is little romance or beauty in the thought of a young woman looking desperately for a place where she could give birth to her first baby. I do not think for a moment that Mary complained, but it is a bitter commentary upon the world that no one would give up a bed for the pregnant woman – and that the Son of God must be born in a stable.

This almost beggarly beginning has been glamorised and romanticised by artists and poets throughout the centuries. Yet I believe that at least once a year we should look steadily at the historic fact, and not at any pretty picture. At the time of this astonishing event only a handful of people knew what had happened. And as far as we know, no one spoke openly about it for thirty years. Even when the baby was grown to be a man, only a few recognised him for who he really was. Two or three years of teaching and preaching, of helping and healing people, and his work was finished. He was betrayed and judicially murdered, deserted at the end by all his friends. By normal human standards this is a tragic little tale of failure, the rather squalid story of a promising young man from a humble home, put to death by the envy and malice of the professional men of religion. All this happened in an obscure, occupied province of the vast Roman Empire.

It is fifteen hundred years ago that this apparently invincible Empire utterly collapsed, and all that is left of it is ruins. Yet the little baby, born in such pitiful humility and cut down as a young man in his prime, commands the allegiance of millions of people all over the world. Although they have never seen him, he has become friend and companion to innumerable people. This undeniable fact is, by any measurement, the most astonishing phenomenon in human history. It is a solid rock of evidence which no agnostic can ever explain away.

That is why, behind all our fun and games at Christmas-time, we should not try to escape a sense of awe, almost a sense of fright, at what God has done. We must never allow anything to blind us to the true significance of what happened at Bethlehem so long ago. Nothing can alter the fact that we live on a visited planet.

We shall be celebrating no beautiful myth, no lovely piece of traditional folk-lore, but a solemn fact. God has been here once historically, but, as millions will testify, he will come again with the same silence and the same devastating humility into any human heart which is ready to receive him.

Let us never be so preoccupied with the tensions and anxieties, or with the rejoicings and celebrations, of this passing world that there is no room in our hearts for the Son of God.

3. CHRISTMAS DAY

No Room at the Inn
"ONCE IN Royal David's City", that is Bethlehem, one thousand nine hundred and sixty two years ago something happened! It was something quite unique in the history of the human race. For GOD, whose vast and complex wisdom science is daily discovering, entered the stream of human history.

When this happened there was no earthquake, no blinding lightning flash, no fanfare of trumpets. When God became man he was born, as all of us were born, as a tiny helpless baby. And he was born in the utmost humility – as the hymn puts it, "in a lowly cattle shed".

I find this a great mystery and a great wonder.

God has been here, on this planet, in person. And so, what we are celebrating today is not the feast of jolly old Father Christmas or of good King Wenceslas, or any kind of beautiful fairy-tale. Behind all the commercialism, all the decoration, all the jollification lies the greatest fact of human history.

It was quiet, you might say – almost unnoticed at the time. But as the years went by and men came to realise what had really happened they changed the very calendar by which we live. We call this year "1962" simply because it is one thousand nine hundred and sixty two years since God entered human life in the person of Jesus Christ. Today is Christ's birthday and we have every right and reason to rejoice.

Of course it is only too easy to romanticise the Christmas story, to sing lovely carols about it, and to smother what really happened under a mass of decorations. But the actual event was far from romantic. There is nothing gay and amusing, you know, about a young woman having to hunt desperately for some shelter when the birth pangs are almost upon her. On that first Christmas morning the world must have seemed a hard place to Mary. At the end of a weary journey there was "no room at the inn". The only shelter offered her was the lowly cattle shed. Nobody thought it worth their while to give up their room at the inn for the Son of God to be born. After all, what was one more expectant Jewish mother to them?

No Publicity

Just consider how such an event might have been planned today! Think of the careful preparation –

the special arrangements – the discreet publicity in the right places beforehand. And then, when the event actually took place and the child was born – the reporters – news coverage all over the world – interviews – special features – microphones – TV cameras!

But God's ways are not our ways. Although this was God entering his own world, he enjoyed no special privilege or protection. As the hymn rightly says, "With the poor and mean and lowly, lived on earth our Saviour holy."

Now it seems to me that the world in which we live today teaches us to value above all things success and wealth and glamour and power. But we shall look in vain for any of these things in the true fact of Christmas. There is indeed a sublime simplicity and a heart-stirring beauty if we look deeply enough. God's wisdom is a far higher thing than ours.

We look, apparently, at a helpless baby, new-born in the humblest surroundings. It *is* hard to believe that he is the Son of God. And yet the longer I live the more I grow convinced that the apparent weakness of Jesus is really a tremendous strength. In the end, whether it is in this world or in the next, it will become plain that there is no true success except in following his way: no beauty without the character that he taught us to follow: and, in the last resort, no power at all except the power of his love. We are quite right to rejoice, to celebrate the birthday of Christ this Christmas morn, but do let us remember what sort of person it is whom we worship. It is one who for humanity's sake was prepared to come down to live at our level, so that he might lift us up to live at his.

God was once himself a Man

The baby was born at Bethlehem, and although it's true, as the hymn says, that the angels of Heaven sang at his birth, very few human beings took the slightest notice. Jesus, the Son of God, lived life on the same terms as all human beings. He was so thoroughly human that his friends were terribly shocked when he began to claim to be the Son of God, and to speak with authority about life and death and the life to come.

Perhaps sometimes we forget how fully human Jesus was. We live on the other side, so to speak, of his triumphant rising from the dead. We didn't know him when he trod the hills and streets of Palestine as a mortal man. We think of Christ as the ascended king in whose hands all power ultimately rests. And we are quite right. But it is a great loss to us if we forget how completely human he was. Some of us find life hard and difficult; perhaps, at times, our burdens seem almost too heavy to bear. But it is precisely then that we need to be reminded that the unseen, but very real, God was once himself a man. He knew temptation; he knew difficulty; he knew ingratitude and disappointment. He saw, far more clearly than any of us, how the heartlessness and stupidity of some people causes suffering to others.

Jesus Christ was a real man – no meek-and-mild nonentity but a man of very great strength. He was angry at the exploitation of the weak by the strong. He said that it would be far better for a man to be dead than for him to harm a little child. He knew the hearts of men, without illusion and without cynicism. And he fully understands your heart and mine.

The True Message of Christmas

Some of us may be haunted by a sense of disappointment and failure. Somehow, we feel, life has cheated us or passed us by. But the life of Jesus Christ, the Son of God, was never a bed of roses. He met with opposition and misunderstanding. He met with the arrogance and hypocrisy of those in privileged places. His mission, which was nothing less than to save the world, ended, in the eyes of the world, as a miserable failure. This Christ, with whom we have to do, knew, at the end of his short life, the bitterness of betrayal by one of his friends and utter desertion by the rest. He knew loneliness; he knew agony of mind and body. He knew the black darkness of being separated from his Father. Yes – he knew the human situation thoroughly, and he knows it now.

Christmas Day reminds us quite simply that God became man. Therefore the one to whom we pray, the one who is by our side and in our hearts, if we will allow him there, is not some vast impersonal power and mind. We are not worshipping and adoring someone who cannot suffer, someone who can never know the burden of pain or anxiety or fear. On the contrary, we are worshipping someone who, of his own free choice, experienced all these things for our sakes.

Once the true message of Christmas dawns upon us our whole picture of God is revolutionised. Whoever we are, wherever we are, there is no disappointment or frustration, no pain or sorrow or failure, which he does not fully understand. When he was on earth he cared particularly for the sick and suffering, the bereaved and the lonely, the unhappy and the outcast. He is the same yesterday, and today, and for ever. You may be certain of his complete understanding and of his unfailing love.

The Call for Compassion

But that is not all. Human life has never been the same again since God became man. Jesus Christ is the living link between man and God, between time and eternity. Since Christ became a man the value of every single human being is enormously increased. Read his teaching for yourself in the four gospels! You will find that he always connected love of God with love of men. He had no use for religion, for prayers or services or anything else, unless they led men to treat their fellows with compassion. He called men to a new way of living, the costly way of outgoing love.

People don't always seem to realise this, but Jesus only gave one picture of the final judgement of all men. In it men are judged – to their astonishment – not by their religious views, not by wealth or fame or success, but by the compassion they showed (or failed to show) to their fellow-men.

Of course it's easy to push aside unpleasant thoughts on Christmas Day, thoughts of those unwanted men, women and children for whom there is still "no room at the inn" – refugees from war and oppression, for example. We can keep these tiresome people with their everlasting problems out of sight – leave them so to speak, "in their lowly cattle shed".

But one day we must all face the one whose birthday we are celebrating today. We have no excuse for not knowing and no excuse for not doing – the call for compassion is all around us. On Jesus' own authority we shall ultimately all be judged by the compassion we have shown, or not shown, to our fellow-men. The day will come when Christ the king will say – "Inasmuch as you have done it to the least of these my brethren you have done it unto me." Or shall we hear him say – "Inasmuch as you have failed to do these things to the least of these my brethren you have failed to do them unto me?"

4. WHEN WE SURVEY

A Meditation for Holy Week

THE SIGNIFICANCE and meaning of the crucifixion of Christ is completely lost upon the non-Christian of today. At his kindliest and most tolerant he sees us Christians working ourselves into a state of pious sorrow over a man who died nearly two thousand years ago, so that we may the better rejoice two days later when we commemorate the same man's miraculous rising from the dead. Today's humanist sees the Christian Church, its members for the most part indoctrinated from early years, perpetuating by every religious device and every appeal to human emotion, a tragedy that is far away and long ago. He cannot see that the death by crucifixion of the field-preacher, Jesus, can really have the slightest bearing upon life as it has to be lived in 1962. It is not because of mere heartlessness or sinfulness that the cross, which is so important to Christians, means nothing to them that pass by. It is far simpler than that: they have not the slightest idea of what the Christian faith really says about God and man.

Faith and Unfaith

Innumerable conversations with hundreds of people over the years have convinced me that most ordinary people have only the haziest idea of what

Christianity is all about. All too often we who are preachers, or writers, or indeed broadcasters, tend to speak to the un-Godded millions as though they were lapsed Christians who, by a few well-chosen words, could be urged back into the fold. The truth is nothing of the kind. The men and women of today have not lapsed from any faith, since they never had one. What they need is not chiding or exhortation, but sheer basic information.

For example, most non-Christians, if sympathetically interviewed, would probably say from their admittedly superficial information that "all religions are the same" since they all want us to lead good lives, be kind to each other, and all promise us a heaven when we die. People are still worshipping, or more probably not worshipping, the most extraordinary magnifications or even distortions of human character, and calling these conceptions "God". It is plain that the revolutionary teaching of the gospel has never been understood, and therefore neither accepted nor rejected.

The Church may be blamed for embalming dynamic truths in out-dated language or in incomprehensible forms; and she may much more be blamed for not giving a far greater share of her attention to the basic modern problem of communication. On the other hand, at least the more intelligent of non-Christians may be held to be at fault for not investigating the historic facts upon which the Christian faith is built. But until we can establish communication between the worlds of faith and unfaith, Calvary will be no more than a dim tragedy of far-off days.

The Christian Faith

The Christian faith says two things about the human predicament which no other religion comes within miles of saying. One is that God, the mind and spirit behind the universe, actually expressed himself in a man. The second is that the value of man is enormously enhanced since God became a human being. In fact, on the authority of the man who was also God, we now know that the way in which we treat our fellow human beings is an accurate reflection of our treatment of God himself.

Let us not smother these two startling, and indeed alarming, assertions of the Christian faith, by wrapping them up in cosily familiar words like "Incarnation" or "Christian charity". The truth is that God has been here on this planet, in person, and has assured us that all men and women, however unimportant or under-developed, are to be treated as his sons and daughters. This is the real Humanism, and only here lies the true worship and love of the living God.

God was in Christ reconciling

Now, if the lonely figure hanging on the Cross so long ago were merely a great and good man, martyred for his beliefs, then that is regrettable, but hardly of any significance to us today. But if it was God who was murdered, if it was God who willingly allowed the forces of evil to close in upon him and kill him, then we are in the presence of something which, though it happened in time, is of eternal significance. We are looking upon something utterly foreign and repugnant to any other religion. We are seeing God allowing himself, not only to be personally involved in the folly, sin and downright evil of the human situation, but accepting death at the hands of his own creatures.

This is a commonplace to Christians, but it is unknown to the majority of people. I believe we must use every skill of communication, every device of writer, artist, poet and dramatist to break the insulation of ignorance and let men see who it is who died upon the cross. We are without doubt in the presence of an incalculable mystery. It is so far beyond the ordinary man's ideas of God, sin, forgiveness and reconciliation that the mind is carried out of its depth and the heart overwhelmed by the dreadful significance of the event. Once people begin to realise that the man on the cross is no demi-god, no puppet-godling, no fragmented piece of godhead, but God himself, there is bound to be an explosion in their thinking.

God who, by definition, is without parts or passions, and has his being independently of time and space, has deliberately put off every supernatural advantage, has willingly embraced the human limitation and at an actual point of time allowed himself to be trapped in the sin-guilt-suffering-death entail of the human race.

"God was in Christ reconciling the world unto himself," wrote Paul, and he was certainly not unaware that these simple words express a mystery which would take a human being all his life fully to comprehend. Yet even the simplest acceptance of what God accomplished, and indeed accomplishes, in the cross of Christ, can lift the pressures of guilt and cause the heart to respond with love and worship. For any man, whether he is yet a Christian or not, can become at times frighteningly aware of his own failures, of his need for forgiveness and reconciliation, both to his own higher self and to his fellow human beings.

I have heard intelligent but agnostic humanists talk of this "sense of guilt" as an inescapable burden which somehow one must learn to live with. But one of the glories of the cross lies in its power to release men from this sense of guilt, in its power to reconcile them to the true and living God. All religions attempt by rite or sacrifice or painful discipline to make atonement, to offer propitiation – somehow to rid man of the burden of his guilt and fear. But this, according to the gospel of our God, has already been done! The reconciliation we are powerless to make, the forgiveness which we can never earn, the taint and the power of past sins which we can never entirely forget – the whole horrible Gordian knot is cut at a stroke by Christ crucified.

The Invincible Power of Love

No one can seriously contemplate God upon the cross with equanimity. This terrible, slow death of all that is good and beautiful is a demonstration in a public place of what our prides and sins are continually intent upon doing, whether privately or in public. This tortured creature, agonised in body, mind and spirit, is the God whom, in our cheaper moments, we accuse of injustice, unlove, and indifference to our human fate. And this, God help us, is the ultimate expression of that vulnerable self-giving love of which the world stands in such desperate need.

This quality, so highly extolled by the philosophers, and so greatly admired by most of us in its milder forms, is seen here in the unlovely gaspings of the dying God. But if in imagination we watch him die, we know the ultimately invincible power of sheer love. What appears to be weakness is really an unconquerable strength. The greatness of God is not really to be known in thunderings and threatenings – it is only too easy for us moderns to see that you have only to increase the amount of terror to brainwash us all! No, it is the lengths to which our God will go to bring us to himself which has moved, and still moves, millions to love and adoration.

An Act of God

But this great tragedy, engineered and accomplished by the wickedness of man, is yet also, strangely, an act of God. No one emerges unchanged from even half-an-hour's contemplation of Calvary. It is soon seen to be not only the divine means of reconciliation, but the divine pattern of redemption. It is an example which, if we are to be of any use at all in the kingdom of God, we must be prepared to follow.

Our crosses are not likely to be Christ's Calvary. But, nevertheless, no situation or relationship is ever permanently changed, and certainly no human personality is ever radically altered, except at the cost of self-giving love. It is nonsensical to suppose that we can achieve anything for the kingdom of God by merely sitting secure in our own salvation. We are called to the same costly involvement in the human situation as was Christ himself. There are religions, fashionable in some quarters, which offer detachment from this passing world and the peace which comes from non-participation in its struggles. But no one could look honestly at the cross and say that this is the way to which we are called. It is true that our roots, our ultimate security, are in the eternal God. But the teaching, the life and death of Christ show quite plainly that we are called to live lives of close human commitment. We are to be Humanists in the name of the Lord our God!

5. GOOD FRIDAY

A Meditation at Golgotha

LET US, with the utmost reverence, use our imaginations for a few moments. Let us see, in our mind's eye, the hill of Golgotha.

The cries of mockery, the jeers and taunts had long since died away. The fearful heat, which had beaten upon the prisoners, pitilessly exposed in their agony, had given place at noon to a sudden chill. For three long hours a strange darkness had covered the countryside. The birds, in this false night, had fallen silent. Many of the onlookers had drawn their cloaks around them in the growing cold and drifted quietly back to Jerusalem.

It was an eery scene. The countryside, usually hard and bright in the sunshine, lay in mysterious shadow. Apart from the Roman guard, very few of either friends or foes of the figure on the central cross still remained. The centurion thought that he had noticed a few of the man's followers stealing back to watch from a safe distance. His own men were restive. They were rough soldiers and, like most rough and tough men, intensely superstitious. They muttered to whatever gods or goddesses they believed in as they shifted uneasily from one foot to another.

The centurion felt a growing conviction that this man on the middle cross was being unjustly, as well as cruelly, executed. No one is put in charge of a hundred men in the Roman Imperial Army unless he is a shrewd judge of men. The other two poor wretches on their crosses were ordinary highway robbers, who would slit your throat as readily as they would slit your purse. They had only got their deserts. But this man – a truly good man if he ever saw one . . . in the name of all that is just and decent never deserved a death like this! Perhaps this darkness was a sign of the wrath of whatever gods there are. He remembered old campaigners of the regiment, who had travelled widely over the vast empire, telling him of similar times of the sun's growing dark in the day-time. Always, he remembered they had told him, the natives had gone nearly crazy thinking that they had mortally offended the gods and that the end of the world had come! But this was none of his business, he reminded himself. His job was to see that the prisoners died, and that no man rescued them. From time to time he spoke sharply to his men, reminding them to keep alert. It was just possible that the followers of this young preacher might seize the opportunity of darkness for a desperate attempt to rescue the man Jesus, although by now he must certainly be almost dead. And then he remembered those followers, and his soldierly lip curled in contempt. For, in the end, when this man had needed them most, they had all fled like the cowards they were.

After three hours of this uncanny darkness the silence was almost complete. At first the jeers and abuse from the bystanders had risen even above the dreadful screams and curses of the agonised thieves. But as time passed and the strength of the victims ebbed, their cries had died down to groans and whimpering. Now, apart from an occasional sighing moan, they hung there silent. The abuse of the bloodthirsty crowd aimed at the man Jesus had died away completely. For one thing he had not answered them back by so much as a word, and after a time even the most brutal will grow tired of fruitless mockery. And then, when the darkness came, and they had made for home, some were even beating their breasts, as Jews were wont to do in times of sorrow. Perhaps there had been something in the dignity and bearing of the central figure, which even transcended the humiliation of his stripped and beaten body, which had touched a heart here and there. When a human heart has raged and railed against a helpless victim, when the fury and the spleen are all spent, there will sometimes come a strange reaction. Perhaps, thought some of those who returned with bowed heads to their homes, it is we who have been shamed, perhaps it is we who are in the wrong.

The centurion glanced up at the three figures. The two thieves, he reflected grimly, are nearly out of it. All their cursing and blaspheming and writhing have exhausted them. But what of this man in the middle? He has wasted no strength, and, despite the dreadful flogging of a few hours ago, he has a strong body.

He may linger until the last beastly business of breaking the legs has to be done. The centurion fervently hoped not. Brave men do not deserve to die like this, and once more the feeling came into his heart that this man was both immensely brave and completely innocent. Perhaps he was even more than an ordinary man, perhaps a son of one of the gods.

This man haunted him strangely. He had asked his God to forgive those who were doing this unspeakable thing to him. He himself had not heard the actual words, but he had seen him speak, probably a few words of comfort, to one of the thieves, even though both of them had been hurling curses at him a few minutes before. And it had been plain that the thief had received some kind of comfort even in his excruciating pain. And then there had been those words spoken to the woman still standing at the foot of the cross, who, he had been told, was the man's mother. It was something about that young man, who is with her now, looking after her and giving her a home. Probably the best he could do, thought the centurion. But, by all the gods, I have never seen any thing like it. Pain of this kind usually brings out the worst in men. They usually curse and scream at friend and foe alike, just as even a favourite dog will turn on his master with bared fangs if the pain is great enough. But not this man. Even in this hell of torture he thinks of others. Once again he had to take a firm hold on himself. A soldier has his duty to do; he is not paid to take sides, except in battle, and he must never allow himself the luxury of pity.

"*My God, My God....*"

And now it seemed to the centurion that the great darkness was beginning to lift. He looked up at the face of the man whose head was still crowned with those wicked spikes of thorn, and he looked hastily away. This was a young man, but the face he had just seen looked as though it had borne every sorrow and pain since the world began. The eyes were open and looking heavenwards. The dry cracked lips moved pitiably, and then, quite suddenly, a great resounding shout came from that man who had been silent for so long. "*Eloi, Eloi, lama sabachthani*" was the cry, and the Hebrew words echoed back from the rocks. This, perhaps the first admission of defeat, the first sign of the cracking of a human spirit, aroused the few cruel mockers who were still on the scene. Evidently they knew as little of the Hebrew tongue as the centurion himself. "Listen," they cried, "he's calling for Elijah! The poor chap's mind's going." Some of them, moved at last by pity, ran to fetch a sponge and some sour wine and a stick so that they could reach the parched lips. But the coarser spirits among them said, "No, let him alone. Let's wait and see if Elijah really does come and rescue him."

But there was, as we all know, no rescue. And those who loved Jesus, even those who watched him at a safe distance, knew the meaning of this cry. It was part of a psalm which they had all known since childhood, and it meant "My God, my God, why hast thou forsaken me?"

"Why didst Thou forsake Me?"

This was the scene, and it may seem a strange moment to introduce the matter of translation and grammar. But I believe it to be of vital importance that we should understand the significance of this question which was shouted "in a great voice" at the end of three hours of darkness. For it need not be interpreted as the cry of a soul lost in the anguish of desolation. The Hebrew words were translated by Mark, or possibly first by Peter, into Greek, and in that language the use of the aorist tense carries naturally the force of "Why *didst* thou forsake me?" I am not a Hebrew scholar but I am told on excellent authority that such a translation is quite in accordance with the sense of the actual words which Jesus spoke. Therefore this strange cry may well have been one of unspeakable relief. The darkness and the desolation had been borne in silence but were now passing away. The dreadful spiritual agony, to which we must return in a moment, had been endured. That cup of suffering which the Son of God had feared and dreaded, and from which he had prayed so desperately to be delivered if it were possible, had now been drained to its last bitter drop. But the experience had been fearful, and the words which came to the mind of Jesus were this direct quotation from a familiar psalm. I believe there is no note of reproach or despair in them, only a shuddering relief as the darkness began to lift. "*My God, my God, why didst thou forsake me?*"

He Asked Questions

With the utmost reverence we must hear this cry again, and try to answer its strange question. But, before we do that, may I suggest to you how characteristic it was of Jesus to *ask a question*, even at such a time. All great personalities have their own peculiar traits, and the greatest of all human personalities was no exception. I wonder whether we have noticed how often Jesus used a question, where we might have expected a statement. The more we love and understand something of his mind the more we see the profound wisdom of his method. When Jesus was asked a question, again and again we find him asking a counter-question, often a haunting as well as a penetrating one, which does its own work as men try to answer it. A few, out of many, examples come quickly to mind. "*Why* are ye so fearful?" he asked the terrified disciples in the storm-tossed fishing boat. And indeed why are you and I so often fearful? To answer that question properly takes us to the very root of our being, to the fundamental relationship between ourselves and God. On another occasion

Jesus said to his enemies, "*Why* go ye about to kill me?" We simply do not know whether his enemies were forced by that piercing question to examine their own hearts. We only know that the more vocal of them hotly protested that they had no murderous intent, even though in fact, they did succeed in getting him put to death. But – and this is a recorded fact which I have found many Christians have overlooked – we read in Acts 6:7 that "a great company of the priests (in Jerusalem) were obedient to the faith". Surely it is highly probable that among these were men whose spirits had been stabbed broad awake by a simple question.

And then there comes into my mind that most remarkable question of all, asked by Christ the Lord, not now on earth but risen and ascended. It was spoken to Saul, the man who had wrought such cruel havoc on the men and women of the early church. What untold damage this one fanatical Pharisee had done! And yet he is brought up short on the road to Damascus, not by any word of condemnation or blame, but in a blinding moment of truth, by a simple question – "Saul, Saul, *why* are you persecuting me?" When it struck the heart of one as fiercely honest with himself as Saul of Tarsus the result was explosive.

I sometimes feel that when we are quiet before the living Christ, he meets us, sinners as we undoubtedly are, not with blame and reproach but with some penetrating question. We must never be so busy with our prayers and devotions that we drown the voice of Jesus. Nor must we be so busy in our lives that we have no time to reply to what he is asking, or to let that reply influence our daily business of living.

So then, this same Jesus had and has a habit of asking questions, the right questions. We find him as a boy of twelve asking questions in the Temple; we find him in his brief but crowded ministry asking questions; and now we find him after the anguish, the loneliness and the despair, asking a question, "My God, my God, why didst thou forsake me?" Surely in the light of what we know of his habit of asking questions, it is neither irreverent nor outrageous to suggest that there was a purpose in the asking of this question too. Those who first heard it must have wondered how to answer it. And we, who are reverently watching the divine Passion nearly 2,000 years later, must surely make some attempt to find an answer.

Why?

Well, let us be plain. Why *did* the perfect man experience not merely physical agony, but that far more deadly thing – the sense of having been deserted by the Father with whom he had enjoyed unbroken communion all his life? I think such answer as we can make must come along two lines.

a). Our Example

First, I honestly believe that the man who is our

example as well as our saviour "was in all points tempted like as we are", but in this instance infinitely more severely. It was the last chance that the principalities and powers from the headquarters of evil would ever have to attack the Son of God. The attacks of the evil one are intermittent – even after the temptation in the wilderness there was a respite. But crowded into these three hours of darkness there was such a concentrated assault of evil, such blackness of soul and such sense of utter dereliction that even the man who had lived his life in perfect faith and obedience cried out as he did when at last it was over.

Surely there is great comfort for us here. There are diseases of the body which produce depression of mind, a phenomenon which many of us have experienced briefly after recovering from influenza or some other virus infection. The colour, the meaning and the point of life temporarily disappear. We pray apparently to an empty heaven, and in our misery we torture ourselves by brutal self-condemnation. Many of us, I repeat, know of these things briefly. But there are those who have to endure such conditions month after month, and even year after year. We who know something of God's love can truly help them by our love and our prayers. There *is* light at the end of their dark tunnel, and in the meantime we may help them far more by our encouragement than perhaps we know.

And, of course, our thoughts go out to those who

are mentally ill. This sickness may be their own fault, or it may be, as far as we can tell, wholly undeserved – it certainly is not for us to judge. But these men and women are going through a hell of darkness and despair. Sometimes those of us who are not experts in the treatment of mental illness can do no more than stand by and pray. It is heartening to remember that such black depression, such utter desolation, fell upon the sinless Son of God. He who is now ascended up on high, taking our humanity with him, as it were, can be relied upon not to have forgotten his own agony. In the popular phrase, "he knows what it's like." And we can pray for those who feel themselves cut off from God in the name of the man who went through the same thing himself.

b). Our Saviour

But the second reason for this unique mental and spiritual agony goes deeper still. Some time before the crucifixion, John the Baptist, with that insight which is the stamp of every true prophet, had exclaimed – "Behold the Lamb of God, which taketh away the sin of the world." Now I cannot pretend even now, after many years in the ministry of the Church, that I understand the mystery of atonement. I only know that the representative man deliberately allowed the evil to make its assault upon him and, in the end, to kill him. Long ago the English hymn-writer Mrs. Alexander wrote:

> We may not know, we cannot tell,
> What pains he had to bear.

I freely confess I do not know, I cannot tell. I only know that what you and I could never do was done for us at infinite cost, upon the cross.

What dreadful truth lies behind the inspired words of Paul when he wrote, "He hath made him to be sin for us, who knew no sin; that we might be made the righteousness of God in him"! It is a brutal statement, and on the face of it desperately unjust. And yet countless millions, down the centuries and throughout the world, have found their relationship with God restored in accepting a sacrifice which they would always be powerless to make. Every time we come to Holy Communion we receive broken bread to represent his sorely wounded body, and poured-out wine to represent the blood which he shed. And this we are commanded to do until he comes again, lest we forget at what a cost the bridge between God and man was built and the reconciliation finally made.

"Right with God"

To some this seems a monstrous, even an immoral, doctrine. How, they ask, can we blithely accept the atoning action of someone else for sins for which we ourselves are responsible? Well, to be blunt, how else can we be "right with God"? If God has not made the reconciliation, who can? Every religion in the world worth serious consideration makes some attempt to remove this dreadful impasse. How can there be reconciliation between the utter perfection of God and the sins and guilt of mankind? A sort of indiscriminate celestial benevolence would no more solve the difficulty than the removal of a man's conscience would solve his own moral problems.

The humanists declare that we have to "learn to live with our sense of guilt" – which shows at least an elementary appreciation of our plight. But the good news says precisely the opposite – we can live *without* that sense of guilt! For what we are powerless to do has now been done, on the initiative and in the person of God himself. All over the world, in almost every country, men and women, who have striven for years with a crippling sense of guilt, have been able to leave their burden at the foot of the cross. This can hardly be dismissed as some sort of mass-deception. Ninety-nine per cent of those who thus accept their forgiveness are not theologians, and probably three-quarters of them could never express in words any consistent theory of atonement. Countless thousands since Paul's day have found their peace in the "atoning work" of Christ. They can only be grateful, as he was, to "the Son of God, who loved me, and gave himself for me".

I am under no illusions about my inability to explain this marvel. We are in the presence of a very great mystery. What, for example, are we to make of Paul's astonishing statement that he (Jesus) "should taste death for every man" or that "God was in Christ, reconciling the world unto himself"? Thousands of books have been written to explain the mystery, and I suppose I must have read hundreds of them. My appreciation of the costly act itself has grown with the years. But I cannot, in all honesty, say that I am much nearer understanding so perilous and costly a mystery.

The more I think of it, the more I allow my imagination to fill in the gaps in the terse Gospel narratives, the less I am surprised that "from the sixth hour there was darkness over all the land until the ninth hour". God only knows what fearful battles were being grimly fought, or what agonies were being silently endured. All that I am certain of is this – the ordeal was endured, the battle was won, and through Christ we are free men who can approach our Father with confidence. But sometimes my blood runs cold when I try to imagine what experience it was which wrung from him the cry, even though it may have been a cry of relief, "My God, my God, why didst thou forsake me?"

6. THE JOY OF EASTER

THE ENEMIES of the Christian faith are inclined to say that the joy of Easter is really nothing much more than the joy of spring! For thousands of years, they tell us, men have had some sort of festival to celebrate the new surge of life in spring. So all we are doing is to tack on to this pagan celebration a story nearly 2,000 years old, and then call it a religious festival!

Now this won't do at all. Obviously, in this country, we can't help connecting the joy of Easter with all the sights and scents and sounds of spring. There's no reason at all why we shouldn't be glad about spring flowers and budding trees and young lambs skipping in the fields. But Christianity is a world-wide religion – and if we lived in Australia, for example, we should now be at the beginning of the autumn and getting ready for the winter. Yet Christians all over the world have a special joy at Easter, whatever the season or climate.

Of course the joy of Easter has a cause much deeper than the renewal of life which Nature shows all over the world at different times. If we look back to the early Church, to the Acts of the Apostles, for instance, we find the chief source of joy is the demonstration of Christ's resurrection. The men who were doubters and cowards before Christ's death are now possessed by a joyful certainty, a certainty about God. Now you don't get much joy out of a legend, however holy, or out of a rather wobbly belief in something that may have happened. You only get a deep joy out of something really good and really true. And that is just what they'd got.

The claims of the man Jesus to be God-in-human-form were proved by the resurrection. Many of the early Christians had *seen* the risen Christ with their own eyes. According to St. Paul, in 1 Corinthians 15, on one occasion he was seen by over 500 Christians at once. And Paul remarks that most of these were still alive at the time of writing, and that was about twenty years after Christ's death. So, obviously, to the early Christians the resurrection of Jesus was fact – *the* fact of human history. They found that the same power which had raised him from the dead could transform them from lives of evil and despair into sons of God, clean, fresh, full of hope. They knew in their bones that Christ was alive *with* them and even *in* them.

And of course that wasn't all. They also knew that death, the terror of the pagan world, had been defeated. For the Christian there was nothing to fear if the body should be destroyed – and they had precious little earthly security those days – they knew that just as surely as Christ had passed through death, so would they.

That was the Easter joy of the early days of the faith. I wonder if we feel the same joyful certainty. I believe that we're infected more than we realise by the anxieties and tensions and fears of today. Secular thinking has made even some of us Christians look at death as though it were the final disaster. But that's nonsense! If our lives belong to Christ our roots are not in this world at all, and our permanent home is not here either. There never has been and never can be lasting security in this little life. Our security is in God and nowhere else.

The joy of Easter is that we know what sort of person God is; that we know the limitless power available to transform us into what we should be; and that we know that death is not the end of living but the gateway to a fuller life with God.

7. THE ABOLITION OF DEATH

The Message of Easter

OF ALL the inspired certainties which sparkle on that sea of confidence in God which is the New Testament, the resounding triumph of Jesus Christ over man's last enemy is perhaps the most magnificent. "Jesus Christ hath abolished death," Paul wrote to Timothy; and what more categorical statement could anyone want than that?

The force of such utter conviction as this is often lost to us simply because of our over-familiarity with the text. Moreover, when we present-day Christians use New Testament expressions we are more often than not borrowing a radiance from the past. We are often merely "quoting texts", but we need to remind ourselves quite sharply that Paul and his fellow-writers were doing nothing of the kind. They were writing truths, which have since become familiar to generations of Christians, *for the first time*.

It is doubtful, for example, if Paul, writing in a dark and unwholesome prison cell, for all his vision, ever for one moment imagined that his words would be used to inspire men and women centuries later. He had no idea that he was writing the Word of God. He wrote out of the conviction, out of the certainty, of his own heart. And as part of his triumphant certainty, in the exuberance of a faith which had become certain conviction, he writes – "Jesus Christ hath abolished death."

This complete abolition of death is, for some reason or other, nearly always accepted with considerable mental reserve, even by experienced Christians. It is true that they hope for resurrection through Christ, and it is true that they believe firmly that the man whose central confidence rests in Jesus Christ will share the timeless life of God. Yet in their minds death, the dark and gloomy old god, the bogey and the terror of so many minds, has somehow still to be passed. But to believe in "the gloomy portal", "the icy river", and all the other forbidding images of which Christian hymn-writers, yes and even authors of the spiritual status of John Bunyan, have written, is without any doubt to refuse to believe in the abolition of death.

But let us imagine for a moment that Paul was exaggerating, that in his triumphant faith in the unseen but real world to which he might at any moment pass, he was forgetting death, the grim and ghastly enemy of all mankind. Suppose in his enthusiasm for the glories and magnificences of heaven he had forgotten what the Anglican Book of Common Prayer so charmingly called the "bitter pains of death." Then let us hear, instead, what Christ said. No one could surely accuse the one who was going to taste death for every man, and an exceedingly bitter death at that, of minimising the actual experience of death itself. Yet what does Christ say? "If a man keep my saying *he shall never see death*" (John 8: *51*). Or again, "And whosoever liveth and believeth in me *shall never die*" (John 11 : *26*). Can these words possibly bear any other interpretation – that death as an experience *does not exist at all* for the man whose life is entrusted to Christ? What other meaning can they bear? And who would dare accuse the one who is himself the resurrection and the life of misrepresenting the facts?

We have grown, God help us, hardened and overfamiliar with the sense-shattering miracle of what we call, in our religious jargon, "the resurrection". We do not feel a thousandth part of its impact, nor do we see a thousandth part of its significance. But the early disciples did. If we had seen, as they saw, the finest and best of men unjustly condemned, and seen him die by inches in the public gaze on Friday; and if we had seen that same man radiantly alive and well and greeting us with his usual friendliness on the following Sunday morning – then we too might have cried out in terror as they did. For though death itself may be a horror to the mind, the sight of a dead man alive again is almost enough to send men out of their senses. Yet when these men saw that this tremendous demonstration of God's power was true, and that the stupendous claims – which for all we know they may have thought were exaggerated – were visibly and tangibly vindicated, their joy knew no bounds. No wonder the early Christians went out to preach "Jesus and the resurrection"! The final enemy, the terror and indeed the torture, of so many minds was shown by unforgettable demonstration to be exploded and defeated.

No, Paul was not exaggerating. He was not carried away by his own eloquence, or indulging in a superior form of wishful thinking. He knew, as all those early believers knew, that death no longer existed; Jesus Christ had abolished it. We may search our New Testaments in vain for any of the gloomy graveyard images, the shadows, the darkness, the pains, the bitterness of death, which still appear in many of our Christian hymns. "To depart and be with Christ, which is far better", "to sleep in Christ", to be "for ever with the Lord" – these are the radiant certainties of the New Testament.

We need firmly to hold on to the fact that there is no death for the Christian; it has been completely abolished. For the old dark god with his weapons of basic, primitive fear still operates, quite illegitimately, in many Christian hearts. We should allow him no foothold, for he has no right to be there, and he has no real power over us. The glory of Easter is not a pious hope that we shall somehow survive after a fear-ridden journey through the "gloomy portal". It is a demonstration of undiluted joy. Christ is the one who bore the sin, the darkness, the terror, and the pain. He is the one who "tasted death for every man".

Hear St. Paul again, writing with infectious holy gaiety: "Christ has forgiven you all your sins: he has utterly wiped out the damning evidence of broken laws and commandments which always hung over our heads, and has completely annulled it by nailing it over his own head on the cross. And then, having drawn the sting of all the powers ranged against us, he exposed them, shattered, empty and defeated, in his final glorious triumphant act!" (Col. 2: *13-15*).

Must we always dim and tarnish the glory of God's magnificent promises with our mental reservations and our secret fears? What stops us from accepting the simple fact that "Jesus Christ hath abolished death"?

8. THE POWER OF HIS RESURRECTION

Physical Power

MAN, BEING a comparatively puny creature upon this planet, has probably always been impressed by physical strength. In the days before machines it was the sheer power of a man's muscles or the great strength of a horse which called forth his admiration, while the savage might of a lion or of a bear filled him with a mixture of awe, delight and fear. There is unquestionably something fascinating about physical strength and power.

As man moved into the age of the machine he began to feel the same fascinated awe towards engines of steam which possessed the power of many thousands of horses. Today it is by no means only the schoolboy who stands admiringly before the controlled might of the express locomotive, or gazes wide-eyed at the giant turbines which drive the ocean-going liner. This sense of awe in the presence of power is common to us all. Who could sit in an airliner and feel the surge and thrust of 10,000 horsepower lifting the vast machine into the air without a kind of exultant reverence for the sheer power under the command of men?

And now the world faces infinitely greater powers, the unleashing of the energy of the very heart of the material universe, the power of the atom. Man's imagination can scarcely grasp what has happened – what fearful power, a million times more potent than anything our grandfathers dreamed of, awaits his harnessing. Whether modern man contemplates the almost unimaginable destructive force of such things as the hydrogen or cobalt bomb, or whether he imagines the vast benefits that the peaceful use of atomic power can bring to human life, he can hardly be blamed for being impressed, as no previous generation has ever been impressed, by the vast new energies which now lie almost at his finger tips.

Spiritual Power

Now there can be nothing wrong in the Christian's feeling this very natural awe in the presence of vast power. But he should not fail to be aware that the power which is most impressive cannot be measured in terms of horse-power, nor can its explosive effect be measured in terms of tons of T.N.T. Let us freely admit that physical marvels are impressive, but let us see quite clearly that they are powerless outside the physical sphere. Not all the atomic energy in the world can alter the fact of man's inevitable death, nor can the most powerful and ingenious machine wield the slightest influence upon a man's inner character. These physical marvels are impotent in the spiritual realm, and are of no use at all against man's real enemies, which are spiritual.

The resurrection of Jesus Christ was to the early disciples not only a vindication of his claims, not only a divine endorsement of his identity, but pre-eminently a demonstration of power. The triumph of the resurrection was conclusive evidence of the vast spiritual power exerted through Christ against those enemies of man which had never previously been defeated – sin and death. In a sense, certainly in a physical sense, Christ went into the long agony which began in the garden and finished on the cross, unarmed and defenceless.

We may be sure that the principalities and powers of hell, seeing him thus exposed, and knowing, as devils do, who he was, made a combined assault upon this man who was also God. We can scarcely guess at the dreadful mystery which lies behind the words of Paul when he wrote boldly that God "made him to be sin for us, who knew no sin." But perhaps we can imagine something of the unspeakable concentration of evil which descended upon the lonely figure on the cross. Yet for all his solitary defencelessness there was sheer spiritual power in that representative man, the power of goodness and love, which the devils habitually under-estimate. When the task was fully accomplished and the fearful burden faithfully borne, God, by spiritual power, raised his Son from the dead. The physical force which moved the stone from the tomb and reduced the tough Roman soldiers to terror was only a trifle, a mere straw in the wind which in its holy blast destroyed the power of sin and death. Can you hear the ring of holy joy behind these exultant words of Paul:

> And then, having drawn the sting of all the powers ranged against us, he exposed them, shattered, empty and defeated, in his final glorious triumphant act.

It was this unforgettable demonstration of power, power released into those dark areas of human being where no man had ever triumphed before, that gave the young Church not only its unshakeable conviction, but also its gay and unconquerable courage. For to them, as surely it should be to us, the resurrection was no mere happy ending to an otherwise ghastly tragedy. It was a demonstration of power, shown once historically in time, on one unique occasion. It was also the birth of a new power altogether, a new weapon and a new resource for the liberation and life of men.

Transforming Power

They knew that this same power, which had triumphed over sin and death, was able to transform human beings, to change them from degraded sinners into shining saints, from miserable cowards into joyful heroes. Previously man's hopes for becoming what he knew he ought to be were defeated by the dead weight of his own past sins, and by his lack of power to rise above them. Moreover, the whole inhabited world was haunted by the dark fear of death. But now – and this is the glory of the Gospel – in one decisive act Christ had drawn the sting of sin, resoundingly shattered the tyranny of death, and made his power available to men.

Some years after the resurrection Paul, in his letter to the Christians at Philippi, is declaring it as his life's ambition to "know him and the fellowship of his sufferings and the power of his resurrection". Surely he does not mean by the last phrase simply that he hopes one day to be lifted from this little life into the fuller life of eternity. For earlier in the same letter, when contemplating his own death, he says in effect that "to depart and be with Christ" (1: *23*) would be as easy as passing from the ante-room into the palace. No, surely what he means here is that he wants to know experimentally the operation of that same spiritual power which raised Christ from the dead. He wants to see more of that power at work in the dark and hard places of his own heart; he wants to see more of that power transforming people in the dark places of the world, such as Rome, Corinth and Ephesus. He has seen by now that the "weakness" in which Christ was crucified is only one side of the immense silently explosive power of love.

Power-starved Men

As we celebrate the joyful triumph of the first Easter – and let us make no mistake about it, it *was* the biggest triumph this world has ever seen – is there not a danger that we forget that that immeasurable super-human power was not turned off somewhere in the first century A.D.? In a world bemused with physical marvels and over-awed by physical power, it is possible for us to be so dazzled as to forget where the human shoe really pinches. We may lose sight of the places where the power is really needed, and in our modern clever age many men may be tempted to think that the old spiritual forces are no longer required.

But which of us, if we are honest and thoughtful, would not have to admit that, both for ourselves and for the rest of sinful humanity, the basic problems are always, in the last resort, spiritual? It is in the realm of the spirit that modern man is so poverty-stricken, so power-starved. It is unthinkable that God ever intended the demonstrated power of the resurrection to dwindle away until it became little more than a revered memory of the past. Could we not share Paul's ambition, and indeed his practice, and dare to tap the resources of God's power? Could we not make a determined effort to strip off the protective insulation of modern ways of thinking, and experience again "the power of his resurrection"?

9. HE ASCENDED UP ON HIGH

Thoughts for Ascensiontide

"*Above the Bright Blue Sky*"

IT HAS always seemed to me that the Ascension of our Lord is something of a poor relation among the festivals of the Church's year. I imagine that this is largely because the divine event is celebrated on a week-day, and unless one is a pupil at a school with Christian observances – when the holy day is chiefly remembered because it is a day's holiday – it is likely to pass almost unnoticed by many good Christian people, and its significance scarcely appreciated.

Paul was not merely uttering a truism when he said – "Now that he ascended, what is it but that he also descended first . . .?" If we really believe that human life was invaded from Heaven by God's becoming a human being, it is surely not unreasonable to believe that the complement to that celestial dive of rescue is an ascension back in triumph to Heaven. The man who was also God had accomplished his mission, he had founded the kingdom, he had effected the reconciliation between God and man, and he had defeated man's last enemy – death. The Ascension not only satisfies the mind by completing the divine work, but it also strengthens and encourages the Christian soul.

Now I believe that an awful lot of nonsense is talked about man's conception of the nature of the world nearly 2,000 years ago. Of course there were ignorant and stupid people then, as there are now, but I find it very hard to accept that people of Paul's education and intellect, for example, believed literally in what is rather impertinently called the "three-storied universe". Certainly they lacked most of the astronomical knowledge which we possess, but I do not think that this means that they thought of "Heaven" as being physically and materially "above the bright blue sky". When, for instance, Paul told the Colossians to "seek those things which are above, where Christ sitteth on the right hand of God" I simply cannot imagine that he visualised some location x miles above the visible display of celestial bodies. Again, when he spoke of being "seated together with Christ" I cannot think that he was speaking of sitting down at some measurable distance above the flat earth! Possibly he is not using the language that we should use, but he is surely thinking of some dimension infinitely beyond and "higher" than the present human situation.

Going "Up"

Men of all religions, or even of none, speak of "high" ideals, "high" aspirations, or even of "high" positions of responsibility or command. This seems to be a normal human trait, even though it is logically absurd, quite as absurd as it is to call one musical note "higher" than another. It does not really matter that the man of prayer might lift up his eyes to the heavens in the northern hemisphere, while the man in the southern hemisphere lifts up his eyes in a completely opposite direction. The point really is that human beings look up to God and what Paul calls the "heavenly", whether they are aware that they live on a spherical globe or not. Thus it was natural for Jesus, his work accomplished, to leave his followers by this acted parable. The man whom the early Christians had seen die and rise again did not simply vanish from their sight, as he had done on several occasions since his resurrection, but visibly ascended. The simplest witness could understand the obvious meaning of this action, while the wisest could ponder long over its deeper significance.

Jesus took Humanity into Heaven

There are two aspects of this, the last earthly action of Jesus Christ, on which I think we can profitably reflect at Ascensiontide. The first is simply this: that Jesus, who was both man and God, was taking humanity in his own person into the heavenly realm. This, naturally, had never been done before. Of course it is true that the risen Christ was not in all respects the same person as the representative man who had died in agony on the cross. We have only to read the resurrection stories to realise this. Yet he had become a man, he had involved himself in the human predicament, and as the eldest of many sons he was taking humanity into the new, perfect world – which is not just another "layer" above the protective belts that lie around this planet, but a new dimension beyond time and space as we know them.

He left with the promise to those who believe in him that "where I am there ye may be also". And since flesh and blood cannot possibly survive in the eternal world, we are promised through the inspired words of Paul that "we shall all be changed" and we shall be given bodies of new quality which the new world will demand. (A fresh reading of the fifteenth chapter of the first epistle to the Corinthians will help our thinking here.)

Jesus prepares a Place for Us

This much I think I can fairly see and believe, and the Ascension of Christ after his triumphant resurrection is the historical guarantee for our faith.

But the second aspect of the Ascension puzzles me considerably. It is simply this: that Jesus Christ, even before his death, spoke of his return to the Father and said these enigmatic words – "I go to prepare a place for you." We cannot help wondering what this preparation could be. We have grown away from the idea, and rightly in my judgement, that Jesus Christ is, to put it crudely, the "cushion" between the angry Father and us sinful human beings. There can be no schizophrenia in the nature of God, and in any case the ascended Christ had made the reconciliation which we could never make. Behind those mysterious and dreadful words, "he hath made him to be sin for us who knew no sin" and "he should taste death for every man", there lies more than a hint of the personal cost of our redemption. But at the time of the Ascension this was over, the agony, the darkness and the dereliction of Calvary had been endured, and the resurrection was the proof that the work was done. What now remains for the ascended Christ to do?

We shall be at Home

I think this promise of Christ's "preparation" for men was meant, and is meant, to convey comfort, love and reassurance. However sincerely we trust our Lord, however deeply we love him, there remains something alarming to the naked human soul who is transferred by death from this familiar sphere into the beauty and perfection of the eternal world. Without in the least subscribing to the Roman Catholic doctrine of Purgatory, as it is popularly set forth, who can doubt that we shall have much to learn when we pass from "here" to "there"? We love and welcome flashes of beauty, truth and goodness, but who in his own imperfection could face their very presence? It is true, as Paul was inspired to write, that "eye hath not seen, nor ear heard . . . the things which God hath prepared for them that love him"; but anyone with any imagination at all can sense the shock to the imperfect when it meets the perfect, to the incomplete when it meets the complete. This is perhaps why we need these words of reassurance.

Without pressing the words too literally, surely we are meant to be both strengthened and reassured by Christ's promise. He who was God by nature became man by deliberate choice, and, having perfected his mission, he now takes the humanity which he shares with us into the world of unimaginable perfection. Whatever lies behind his mysterious promise of "preparation" surely he means that we shall be at home in the place which he has prepared. We may be amazed but we shall not be terrified; we may be dazzled but we shall not be blinded. And it is perfectly possible that the tears which God will wipe from our eyes will not only be tears of regret for our past failures but tears of joy and unspeakable relief.

I spoke above of Ascension Day having become a kind of poor relation. It should, in fact, remind us that in our Lord and Saviour we have an infinitely rich relation! For he is rich in mercy, in love and in understanding. He has defeated all our enemies, and the welcome which he has prepared for those who love and trust him will certainly surpass our wildest dreams.

www.ingramcontent.com/pod-product-compliance
Lightning Source LLC
Chambersburg PA
CBHW070315230426
43663CB00011B/2137